Better Homes and Gardens®

Basements

YOUR GUIDE TO PLANNING AND REMODELING

Better Homes and Gardens® Books
Des Moines, Iowa

Better Homes and Gardens® Books
An imprint of Meredith® Books

Basements: Your Guide to Planning and Remodeling
Editor: Paula Marshall
Writer: John Riha
Designer: Michael Burns
Associate Art Director: Lynda Haupert
Copy Chief: Catherine Hamrick
Copy and Production Editor: Terri Fredrickson
Contributing Copy Editors: Carol Boker, Marty Miller, Diane Witosky
Contributing Proofreaders: Kathy Eastman, Steve Hallam, Margaret Smith
Contributing Illustrators and Designers: Carson Ode, The Art Factory
Electronic Production Coordinator: Paula Forest
Editorial and Art Assistants: Kaye Chabot, Mary Lee Gavin, Karen Schirm
Production Director: Douglas Johnston
Production Manager: Pam Kvitne
Assistant Prepress Manager: Marjorie J. Schenkelberg

Cover photograph: Doug Smith. Cover styling: Wade Scherrer. Wicker furniture from the Melbourne Collection, courtesy of Pier One. Photos courtesy of: Judy Slagle, pages 20-21, 39, and 45. Alise O'Brien, pages 6-7 and 49.

Meredith® Books
Editor in Chief: James D. Blume
Design Director: Matt Strelecki
Managing Editor: Gregory H. Kayko
Executive Editor, Shelter Books: Denise L. Caringer

Director, Sales & Marketing, Retail: Michael A. Peterson
Director, Sales & Marketing, Special Markets: Rita McMullen
Director, Sales & Marketing, Home & Garden Center Channel: Ray Wolf
Director, Operations: George A. Susral
Vice President, General Manager: Jamie L. Martin

Better Homes and Gardens® Magazine
Editor in Chief: Jean LemMon
Executive Building Editor: Joan McCloskey

Meredith Publishing Group
President, Publishing Group: Christopher Little
Vice President, Consumer Marketing & Development: Hal Oringer

Meredith Corporation
Chairman and Chief Executive Officer: William T. Kerr
Chairman of the Executive Committee: E. T. Meredith III

All of us at Better Homes and Gardens® Books are dedicated to providing you with information and ideas you need to enhance your home. We welcome your comments and suggestions about this book on basements. Write to us at: Better Homes and Gardens® Books, Do-It-Yourself Editorial Department, LN116, 1716 Locust St., Des Moines, IA 50309–3023.

Contents

Evaluate
Q&A

Encouraging answers to the most frequently asked questions about basements.

If you need more living area, you may need to look no further than under your feet. Your basement is fully enclosed, complete with walls, a floor, and a ceiling. Best of all, it's space you already own—there's no need to construct an expensive addition or move to a new house to gain a family room, an extra bedroom, or a hobby area.

You can convert most unfinished basements to living space with a minimum of effort and cost, provided the area is dry and in good repair. A little creative thinking quickly dispels the notion of basements being perpetually damp and gloomy. Add windows, lighting fixtures, and personal touches to make the space cheerful, bright, and inviting.

Before you begin, you'll need to know if your basement meets certain basic code requirements, if it will remain free of moisture problems, and how much work will be required to complete your ideal project. The following questions and answers will help you to determine what you'll need to do to make your basement a great living space.

> ▶ *With its coffered ceilings, sophisticated furnishings, and attractive fireplace, this walkout basement is no longer a gloomy, discouraging space. Simple but clever design ideas, such as hiding the necessary ductwork in the ceiling, transformed this basement into an exceptional living area.*

How can I tell if my basement is dry enough to be a living area?

This is often a homeowner's primary concern about basement living. You'll want to be sure that your basement is dry and stays that way for many years. Some problems are obvious—wet or damp walls, telltale moisture stains on floors, and periodic flooding are sure signs that corrective measures are required before any work can proceed.

Water is particularly tricky to control and can invade a basement in a variety of ways: excess rainwater in the surrounding soil forcing its way through foundation walls, rising water tables permeating unsealed concrete floors, and condensation forming on pipes. Many moisture problems originate around the exterior of the home and can be fixed with preventive maintenance or drainage systems. Others require professional expertise. For a complete explanation of how water gets in basements—and how to keep it out—turn to "Keeping Basements Dry," beginning on page 54.

➤ *This basement has a great open feeling. The stairway has no risers behind the treads, and the area underneath is left open to allow a full view from one side of the room to the other. A reflective ceiling helps direct light around the interior.*

▶ *When planning this new home, the owners decided to put their master bedroom in the walkout basement. An inviting—but private—patio outside sliding glass doors helps turn this suite into a cozy retreat.*

My basement ceiling seems low. How do I know if I have enough headroom?

Most building codes require a basement room to have a minimum ceiling height of 90 inches (7 feet, 6 inches) for at least half of the room. Some exceptions include bathrooms, kitchens, and hallways, which can have ceiling heights of 84 inches (7 feet). Measure the distance between the floor and the bottom of the ceiling joists to determine if there is enough room for creating a new living area. Your plans may call for modifications to the existing floors or ceilings, such as installing a new insulated floor or a sound-proof ceiling system. If so, you'll need to allow for these thicknesses when you make your measurements.

Codes also dictate that rooms designed as living areas (as opposed to bathrooms or laundry rooms) must have at least 70 square feet. This includes no less than 84 inches of horizontal space in any direction. By this standard, a wall less than 7 feet long would not meet code requirements. While it may be easy to find 70 square feet of usable space in your basement, the practicality of the space will be determined by the kinds and sizes of the furnishings you need to include.

> *Stud partition walls insulated with fiberglass batts join with carpet squares to help keep this exercise room quiet. (Some commercial carpet squares simply lie atop a concrete floor with no gluing required.) The suspended, acoustical ceiling tiles also absorb noise.*

My basement walls have some cracks. Will I need to repair them before I can remodel my basement?

Soil movement and settling around the foundation exerts pressure on even the sturdiest basement walls, causing cracks. While minor cracks do not threaten the integrity of the foundation, they indicate drainage problems around the house that you should correct before finishing the basement. Cracks also can be a source of moisture or radon gas leaks (see page 10).

Using the guidelines found in Chapter 4, "Keeping Basements Dry," you should fix any drainage problems around the perimeter of your house. This should relieve pressure on foundation walls and prevent further cracking. Existing cracks

■ *Turn a basement into a home theater with a big-screen television and sleek black laminate cabinetry* (above and right). *To give the illusion of spaciousness, the built-ins stretch from wall to wall and floor to ceiling. The ceiling is clad in reflective panels.*

should then be sealed from inside using hydraulic cement and the techniques described on page 60.

Severe bowing of basement walls may require steel bracing installed inside the walls. In this situation, consult a licensed building or remodeling contractor who specializes in basement repair. Find these professionals in the Yellow Pages of your telephone directory under "Foundation Contractors" or "Waterproofing Contractors." Always ask for references before selecting a contractor (see page 110).

Q. *I've heard that radon gas is present in some basements. How can I tell if it is a problem in my house?*

Q. *My basement is gloomy and lightless. How can I make the space livable?*

A. Radon is an odorless, colorless gas that occurs naturally in many types of soil and is often present in negligible amounts in basements. Because it has been linked to lung cancer, however, high levels of radon are considered a serious health threat. Most hardware stores or home improvement centers have do-it-yourself kits that will measure the approximate radon level in your basement. For best results, be sure to follow the directions of your kit precisely.

If your kit indicates high levels of radon, seek the advice of a trained technician. These experts are listed in the Yellow Pages of your telephone directory under, "Radon Mitigation" or "Radon Testing." First, a radon technician will install sensitive instruments that may need to remain in place for several months to give accurate readings of the amount of radon gas present. Based on the results, an expert in mitigation will offer appropriate solutions to your radon problem. The most common solutions include sealing cracks and joints between walls and floors. Correcting severe radon problems may require installing a system of fans and ducts to vent air to the outside and introduce fresh air to the basement. Depending on the extent of the problem and size of the basement, expect to pay between $250 and $3,000 for expert radon mitigation.

A. Basements are much like any other living space in your home. You can finish, paint, and decorate them in any way you choose. If adding natural light is one of your goals, consider installing above-grade windows or window wells that provide excellent daytime lighting (see page 50, "Adding Windows"). Also, you can install any type of artificial lighting, including recessed ceiling lights, wall sconces, indirect perimeter lighting, or freestanding fixtures (see

▼ *Unused basement space became a live-in display for this collector of 1950s memorabilia. Creating a soffit around the perimeter of the space made room for ducts, wires, and pipes. A false wall accommodates a row of glass bricks that can be illuminated from behind.*

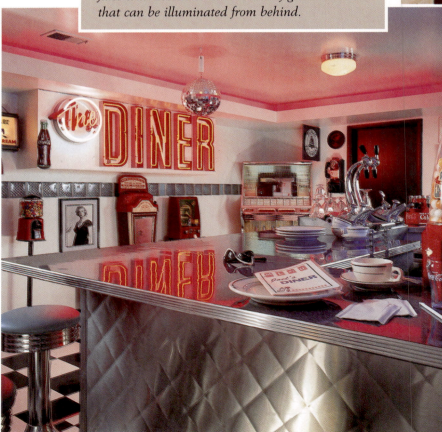

pages 70-71, "Lighting"). Basements are especially good locations for home theaters—a use that does not require a good deal of available daylight.

Furnishings, too, can lighten and brighten a potentially dark basement. Consider vibrant-hued upholstery colors and lightly stained or painted wood finishes. See-through glass-topped tables, touches of airy wicker, and seating pieces with exposed arms or legs add a more-spacious feeling.

For warmth and cozy ambiance, nothing beats a new fireplace. You can install gas fireplaces in most basement locations, but wood-burners are possible, too (see pages 74–75, "Fireplaces").

Is it possible to install a bathroom in my basement?

If you have the headroom required by building codes—usually 84 inches—you may consider a bathroom in your plans. However, it can be tricky to add the drain necessary for a shower or a toilet. The installation of either of these fixtures means connecting to an existing main drain. This may determine the location of the bathroom and require cutting and removing concrete to splice into the existing drain line—a potentially messy and expensive job. One solution is to elevate the new bathroom to create under-foot space in which to conceal new plumbing lines and a drain. Just be sure that the room will still have a ceiling height of at least 84 inches. Because of these complex issues, seek the advice of a qualified building contractor, remodeling specialist, architect, or plumbing professional before beginning your plans. See pages 68-69 for more on planning a basement bathroom.

If you're building a new house and would like to consider an additional bathroom for the future expansion of your unfinished basement space, be sure your builder understands your plans and provides the necessary plumbing roughed in at the proper locations. It's much easier—and much less expensive—to provide for your future plumbing needs now than to add them after concrete floors are poured and foundation walls built.

➤ *Separated from the family living area by a low wall, this basement office is both private and accessible. Acoustical panels in the suspended ceiling help reduce ambient noise from other areas within the home.*

▲ *Classic furnishings and a monochromatic color scheme add sophistication to a walkout basement that was designed to serve as a major part of this home's living area. Well-spaced recessed lighting, supplemented by reading lamps and chandeliers, banishes any subterranean gloom.*

If I make my basement into a living area, do I need to plan for an escape exit? And, does that same rule apply to a basement bedroom ?

The rules are different for living and sleeping spaces. Building codes do not require you to provide an escape exit *unless you intend to create a bedroom in your basement*. In that case, the bedroom must have an exit, usually a window, with an opening that is no less than 5 square feet, with a minimum width of 24 inches. This opening, called an *egress window*, allows a person to escape in an emergency. To make it readily accessible, the lower edge of the window opening must be no more than 44 inches from the floor. For more on installing an egress window, turn to pages 50-52, "Windows and Doors."

Using Your Basement

A surprisingly flexible space, the basement provides room for several options.

Deciding how you'll use your basement space is the first step in developing project plans. Your options are plentiful—basements can accommodate almost any household activity—but choose wisely to keep budget down and usability high.

You and your family likely have several ideas about how to use your basement space. Perhaps you've always wanted an exercise area big enough for two, a nook just for wrapping gifts, or an activity room for busy teenagers, complete with big-screen television, stereo equipment, and a small kitchen for preparing snacks. Many basements are large enough to accommodate a variety of needs, but careful planning is the key to getting the best results. If your budget allows, hire a design professional, such as an interior designer or an architect, to help you plan successfully.

On the practical side, each use has different requirements for accessibility, lighting, energy efficiency, sound insulation, building code compliance, and other factors. Assess pertinent details as you consider each use to get maximum results for your space—and investment.

Sometimes, what's really wanted is a whimsical space: a room made to look like a diner from the 1950s, or a home theater that appears to open to the stars. Basement projects often encourage the adventurous side of home design. They're great spaces for indulging a dream or displaying an extensive collection, greatly increasing your enjoyment of your home.

▶ *If you're into nostalgia, consider a scheme that begins with '50s-style knotty pine paneling and ends with a crackling fire. Comfortable seating pieces clad in plaid create an especially cozy place to sit, relax, and share conversation. Lamps and recessed lighting combine to keep this area bright.*

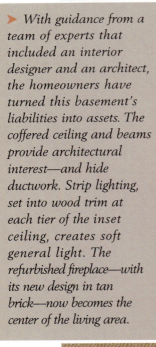

▶ With guidance from a team of experts that included an interior designer and an architect, the homeowners have turned this basement's liabilities into assets. The coffered ceiling and beams provide architectural interest—and hide ductwork. Strip lighting, set into wood trim at each tier of the inset ceiling, creates soft general light. The refurbished fireplace—with its new design in tan brick—now becomes the center of the living area.

A Fabulous
Family Room

Creating a new family room is a great way to increase the all-purpose living space for the entire family. Equipped with a television, stereo equipment, bookshelves, and a few pieces of comfortable furniture, even a small basement family room can substantially increase the livability of your home. If you stick with a basic plan, this is one of the easiest conversions for a basement—you don't have to plan for special considerations, such as plumbing, closets, or egress windows. The main concerns are keeping the space dry and selecting finishes for walls, floors, and ceilings.

When planning a family room, keep flexibility in mind. How do you live? Should the space handle a variety of family activities, from watching movies and playing board games to housing a boisterous birthday party? Do you want a quiet escape for reading and music listening? If your answer is "yes" to all of the above, choose comfortable furniture that you can easily rearrange. Stackable storage units with doors keep toys and games handy but out of sight. Modular seating pieces offer many options as your needs change. And, movable floor and table lamps let you put light where you need it.

For maximum usability, plan plenty of electrical outlets, two or three cable television outlets at various points around the room, and at least two phone jacks—one for the telephone (so that you won't have to scurry upstairs each time the phone rings), and another for a computer modem hookup. Having options for connections will allow you to rearrange furniture at a later time, if desired.

See Also:
"Floors" and "Walls," pages 38–45
"Lighting," pages 70–71

A Private
Bedroom
Retreat

The minimal natural light, coolness, and quiet make basements perfect places for sleeping retreats. Start by considering size. A good size for a bedroom is a minimum of 125 square feet to accommodate a double bed and 150 square feet for two twin beds.

Address code requirements to ensure the safety of your basement bedroom. A wall-mounted light switch, immediately inside the door, often is required by code. And, you must provide direct access to the outside in case of fire or other emergency. This requirement, called *egress*, specifies a window or a door that opens from the inside and has an unobstructed opening of at least 5 square feet. If your basement is not a walkout, then planning for an egress window or door is a primary consideration.

Basements tend to stay cool in summer, so air conditioning may be unnecessary. However, there should be a source of heat. Electric space heaters, wall heaters, and baseboard units are all easily installed and provide inexpensive heat sources. Gas-fired or kerosene appliances must meet local code requirements and should not be used if they don't comply. Install a smoke alarm outside the bedroom door and another over the stairway. If your furnace and water heater are in the basement, be sure to install a carbon monoxide alarm, too.

To create a comfortable bedroom environment, you should completely finish the walls, floor, and ceiling. A fully insulated floor may not be necessary, but covering the concrete with carpeting will greatly increase the room's comfort. Fiberglass insulation between ceiling joists quiets the sound of footsteps overhead. Shrubbery or a fence in front of windows screens the view from the outdoors.

See Also:

"Sound Insulation," page 49
"Windows and Doors," pages 50–53
"Heating & Cooling," pages 66–67

◄ *This guest bedroom, located in the walkout basement of a new house, has a spacious look thanks to 10-foot-high, poured-concrete basement walls. The taller walls cost about 10 percent more than a standard, 8-foot-high basement wall. Even in a standard basement, a lofty poster bed can add a feeling of spaciousness.*

Basement Offices See The Light

Conveniently separate from the main living areas of your house, basements readily accommodate home offices in space that's private and quiet. Primary requirements for an office are light; heat; sufficient electrical wiring to handle computers, fax machines, and printers; and communications service for both a telephone and a computer.

Adding stud walls provides the space to run new wiring. Because existing wiring is typically exposed in the overhead joists, it's easy to extend an electrical circuit or add a telephone jack. But adding a separate circuit to isolate your computer and other office equipment from power to the rest of your home is a smart idea. Drawing too much power from a single circuit can trip circuit breakers and cause the loss of valuable information. Consult with a licensed electrician about adding a new circuit. Allow enough electrical outlets so you can move equipment around or change the design of your office scheme.

Proper lighting is important for anyone spending long hours working in an office environment. Include two types of lighting. Ambient light is the soft, diffuse light that illuminates the whole room. It comes from sources such as ceiling fixtures and daylight through windows. You even can make window-less space more habitable by using what's called *full-spectrum light bulbs*. These have a light spectrum similar to natural sunlight. Task lighting is flexible and can be directed where you need it. A desk lamp is a good example.

Install a portable dehumidifier. High humidity can slow the drying time of documents printed on inkjet printers, causing them to smear. It also can ruin books and other documents.

Basement floors are usually cool in all seasons, especially winter, so consider an insulated floor to prevent your feet and legs from becoming uncomfortably chilled while you're working in your office. For more on insulating floors, see page 40.

▶ *Thanks to careful planning—right down to the size and location of the desk—a metal support post seems to disappear from this thoughtfully designed basement office scheme.*

See Also:

"Floors" and *"Walls,"* pages 38–45
"Lighting," pages 70–71

➤ *With storage shelves and task lighting, this desk doubles as a hobby center. The stacked cardboard containers on top of the shelf unit hold craft supplies. An ergonomically designed chair allows hours of comfortable sitting.*

Time for **Play**

Kids need space to play, and basements are ideal. You can devote an entire area to your child's play needs without disrupting household routines, and space is plentiful for large objects such as art tables or train sets. Add storage for the games, toys, and books that children collect as they grow.

Clever color combinations, durable wall and ceiling treatments, and comfortable flooring appeal to youngsters and make the space uniquely theirs. If walls are in good repair, you don't have to finish them with anything but a coat of paint in kid-pleasing colors. Select flooring materials that are easy-to-clean. You can install vinyl tiles directly over concrete slabs, adding inexpensive dashes of color and providing flat surfaces ideal for stacking blocks and playing with wheeled toys. For older children, consider a softer, stain-resistant carpet.

Be sure there's plenty of light. Recessed ceiling fixtures are ideal—they provide adequate light but don't protrude into the play area where they can be bumped. Track lighting is inexpensive and installs directly on ceiling surfaces.

Basement stairs should have handrails on both sides. Stairways with open sides should have spindles or slats installed to fill the space. The spaces between spindles should be no wider than 4 inches. Sources of heat, such as baseboard heaters, should not be located behind furniture where paper, fabric, or other flammable objects can get wedged against them.

See Also:
"Floors," pages 38–41
"Heating & Cooling," pages 66–67
"Lighting," pages 70–71

◄ *Give kid's spaces a bold, high-contrast scheme the affordable way. Tough sheet vinyl flooring teams with block walls painted cotton-candy pink to set a playful mood. A tented fabric ceiling hides pipes and helps absorb noise. Ceiling how-to tips begin on page 46.*

▲ *With its raised floor and decorative canvas panels, this home theater center doubles as a stage where kids can perform. The back panels—suspended from ceiling tracks—close to hide the TV and create a backdrop for kiddie theatricals.*

Media Mogul

Because you can easily darken basements for a theaterlike effect, they make ideal family entertainment rooms. Along one wall, you can dedicate space for a big-screen or projection television, surround-sound system, and movie playback equipment such as VCRs and laser disc machines. Plenty of overstuffed sofas, chairs, and ottomans will make the spot a favorite, both for family gatherings and entertaining friends.

Hang curtains over walls to control sound transmission, or cover the walls with a sound-absorbing material, such as corkboard. Insulate between exposed overhead floor joists with fiberglass batts, then cover the ceiling with ½-inch drywall. For extra sound insulation, install drywall on resilient metal channels designed especially to increase

sound absorption, or install an acoustical tile ceiling system. Carpeting the floor also helps muffle sound.

Include an indirect lighting system for soft, ambient light without on-screen glare. You can create indirect light by placing fixtures inside a wood frame that runs around the perimeter of the room. Light is cast toward the ceiling, where it is diffused and reflected. Place light fixtures on dimmer switches for maximum control.

Projection devices usually are suspended from the ceiling, so plan a location where the device won't bang heads. Placing a piece of furniture, such as a coffee table or end table, under the projector will detour foot traffic and help prevent accidents.

If space and budget allow, add a "concession stand" for your family's enjoyment. Include a small refrigerator to keep beverages and other refreshments handy. Some refrigerator models are made specifically to fit underneath standard-height counters. You can complete this area with a mini-microwave oven for making popcorn or warming nacho dip and other snacks.

See Also:

"Sound Insulation," page 49
"Lighting," pages 70–71

▲ *This basement home theater features a projection television linked to a digital satellite system. Surround-sound speakers are hidden behind the black fabric panels, and the walls are covered with sound-absorbing panels.*

Exercise: A Way of Life

Exercise equipment stored in the living area of a home often is ignored—witness the popular stationary bike/clothing rack combination or the dusty treadmill tucked into a corner. Given a space designed specifically for this purpose, you're more likely to exercise regularly. Converting basement space into an exercise room is relatively easy because little, if any, mechanical work is required.

Create a workout environment suited to your style, whether it's quiet and meditative, or set to sight and sound. If you're adding 2x4 walls, run the wires and cable for stereo or television before covering them with drywall. Fixing a television to a swiveling, ceiling-mounted corner bracket allows you to view the set from anywhere in the room.

Install tough, durable flooring—vinyl and rubber tiles are good choices. To help you evaluate your workout techniques, use lightweight, shatterproof acrylic mirror panels on the walls. Plan the space on paper first, and provide corridors with a minimum of 30 inches between pieces of equipment. You can use the "Room Arranging Kit," beginning on page 90, to try out various options before any work begins.

See Also:
"Floors" and *"Walls,"* pages 38–45
"Lighting," pages 70–71

◄ *Rather than curse the darkness, the owners of this workout area dug out the ground outside their basement walls, then installed greenhouse windows, (far left). This strategy works especially well if the excavation is on the sunny south side of the house. Inside, touches of red paint and golden pine warm up a potentially cool, white space.*

Relax in a Hot Tub or Sauna

A basement is the ideal location for a hot tub or a sauna. When installed inside the home, be aware that hot tubs and saunas have special requirements.

Hot Tub

A basement works well for a hot tub because the concrete slab floor requires no additional structural reinforcement to handle the considerable weight—even a modest-size tub can weigh more than 4,000 pounds when filled with water. Electrical and plumbing systems, however, need to be adapted to handle the load. You'll need a dedicated electrical circuit to supply your tub with the power it needs to heat and recirculate water, and to run whirlpool jets. A licensed electrician should be consulted to evaluate your home's electrical system and determine the best way to provide power to the tub's heater and controls.

You'll also need water supply lines to fill the tub, and a drain to empty it. The hot tub's drain must be tied into your home's main drain line—a project that may require cutting into your basement floor to access the main line. The location of the main drain can limit the location of your tub. In order to obtain the necessary clearance underneath the tub for the drain line, it may be possible to install it on a raised platform. You should consider these restrictions and options when you discuss the installation of a hot tub with a professional plumber.

The walls surrounding a hot tub will be exposed to excessive humidity, so select moisture-resistant finish materials such as ceramic tile or redwood paneling. Install them over moisture-resistant drywall, also known as *green board*. For a painted finish, use a high-quality paint that is designed to withstand moisture and is resistant to mildew and mold.

Excessive moisture can migrate into the floor overhead where, over time, it can encourage mold growth underneath carpets and carpet pads. To prevent moisture from migrating upward, you can create a vapor barrier by covering ceilings with 4 mil polyethylene. Then install green board before applying finish materials.

Hot tubs are made in various sizes and depths. A typical unit is 5 to 6 feet in diameter and has a depth of 3 to 4 feet. They often are manufactured as one-piece units made of acrylic or fiberglass. You'll need to make sure you have adequate access to your basement in order to install a large hot tub.

Sauna

Saunas usually come as prefabricated packages that include the interior walls, floor, and ceiling materials, as well as the heater and its controls.

Saunas use dry heat, so no water supply or drains are required. Most saunas have no special electrical requirements. You can readily tie a heater and its controls to existing household circuits.

You'll need to construct a shell that consists of 2x4 walls with a door. For energy efficiency, insulate the walls with fiberglass batts and install an exterior-type door. If the shell butts against overhead joists, insulate the spaces between the joists. Closely follow the manufacturer's directions for construction of the shell. As a fire precaution, building codes usually require the shells to have drywall applied to both exterior and interior surfaces. Use moisture-resistant green board to cover the inside of the walls.

Before construction, make sure that walls and floors are level and plumb. Basement floors often slope toward a central floor drain, so you may need to compensate for the slope with shims. Once the shell is constructed, finish materials such as spruce, cedar, or redwood are applied to the interior. Some sauna kits include all materials, even the shell. Such units are designed for outdoor use, but they can be adapted to interior installations. You will need to measure carefully to ensure that the completed package fits in your basement.

See Also:

"Floors" and "Walls," pages 38–45
"Bathrooms," pages 68–69

➤ *The basement enclosure for this 500-gallon redwood hot tub is covered with moisture-resistant cypress paneling. Louvered entry doors encourage air circulation. Ductwork for the home's heating and cooling system, which runs along the back wall just below the ceiling, was enclosed with a combination of cypress and drywall.*

Laundry Centers
Make Clean Getaways

Moving your washer and dryer to the basement keeps the inevitable tangle of clothes and noise from disrupting everyday life. Increase efficiency by including moisture-proof surfaces and plenty of storage in your plan.

A typical laundry hookup requires hot and cold water supply lines and a drain system, items readily accessible in a basement. Often, laundry wastewater is directed to a large sink or tub positioned directly over a floor drain. A floor drain in a laundry center is also a good idea in case of spills, or if

▲ *The desk and painting of a window dress up an otherwise blank space in this laundry room.*

◄ *To eliminate tiresome bending to retrieve clothes, the owners raised this dryer on an 8-inch-high platform made of plywood. The convenient wardrobe hanger folds flat against the wall when not in use.*

a malfunctioning washing machine needs to be emptied of water before it can be serviced. If no floor drain is convenient to the laundry, the wastewater drain needs to be connected directly to your home's drain system. It's advisable to leave the calculations necessary to determine the proper angle and length for drainage pipes to a professional plumber.

Choose water-resistant, durable materials for laundry room floors. Glue-down sheet vinyl is a tough, inexpensive material. If the concrete slab is

▲ *A cabinet with a sink and laminate top provides a great spot for folding clothes or repotting plants.*

▲ This laundry center has a stacking washer and dryer to save space, closets for storage, and a fold-down ironing board, all with hideaway doors. There's even a tub enclosure.

free of cracks and chips, painting with a top quality, water-resistant enamel is an inexpensive and practical way to cover the floor.

Consider adding features that improve convenience and usability. These touches may include a base cabinet with a laminate countertop for folding clothes, a sewing center, a built-in ironing board, or a laundry chute connected to an upstairs hallway or bedroom. Or, include space for completing craft projects that require paint or other messy materials since laundry rooms are excellent cleanup centers.

▲ A niche for craft projects includes a few cabinet drawers devoted to paint supplies.

Good Work
Down Under

The isolated nature of basement space is a distinct advantage when creating a home workshop.

Power

Providing adequate power is a key concern for shops with power tools. You may need to add one or more separate electrical circuits to accommodate the load. Have these circuits routed through a subpanel installed on a shop wall so that circuit breakers are handy. For an extra measure of safety, use a master switch located at the subpanel to turn off power to all equipment when the shop is not in use.

Dust and Noise

Woodworking shops generate plenty of dust. Install a dust-collection system to keep it under control. Without one, dust will find its way into the forced-air heating and cooling systems and settle throughout the house. Have vacuum hoses connected to every piece of equipment.

Install weather stripping on doors for dust and noise control. Shops also need good ventilation. Provide at least two operable windows and a fan for removing fumes. And, add sound insulation to keep shop noises from disturbing the rest of the house.

Lighting and Access

Good lighting is essential. Install fluorescent fixtures at regular intervals along the ceiling for general lighting and work lights for specific tasks. Paint walls and ceilings light colors to reflect light.

Either paint floors or cover them with sheet vinyl for easy cleaning. To prevent muscle fatigue from standing on concrete, place rubber mats at key locations throughout your shop.

Carefully consider how you will move materials and equipment in and out of your shop. You may have to modify stairs or install passage doorways at least 36 inches wide to allow full access.

▶ *This home shop is installed in a typical 12x16 basement area with a 7-foot, 6-inch ceiling height and two small, above-grade windows. The walls are partially covered with perforated hardboard that supports hangers and organizers to keep tools and supplies within easy reach. Wall-hung storage cabinets mount on support strips so the cabinets can be lifted from their supports and moved to new locations. To clear fumes and remove dust, a fan operates in one of the windows, and every piece of equipment is connected to a dust-collection system.*

Room for Active Families

If you need more space for the expanding recreational needs of a growing family, you'll find a basement activity center can serve many purposes all at the same time. Perhaps start with a television in one corner, a pool table in the middle of the room, and a snack bar against a wall. Add storage for toys and games, being sure to leave plenty of floor space for play. Then bring in a few pieces of exercise equipment. Basement rooms can accommodate almost any pastime, often several at once.

Make the space inviting and banish boredom with a lively decorating scheme. The basement is separated visually from the rest of the house, so you can use different—or bolder—color-palettes without fear of clashing

The first step is eliminating water and installing the necessary equipment to keep the space dry (see "Keeping Basements Dry," Page 54). If possible, install or enlarge windows. Even small openings provide daylight, ventilation, and greatly enhance the value of your basement living area. If even small windows aren't possible, you may want to try using full-spectrum light bulbs that mimic natural sunlight.

Plan for flexibility. Install plenty of electrical outlets, phone jacks, and recessed ceiling lights so you can rearrange the space as the needs of your family change.

◄ Each of the family members in this home had a special wish list for the new living area. The teenage son wanted a place to entertain friends and play his favorite game—pool. The father wanted an exercise area with a television. The mother—an interior designer—wanted to indulge her personal taste for a no-holds-barred decorating scheme. All their wishes were granted in this 600-square-foot basement.

Refining the **Space**

Address the special needs of basement surfaces, and provide light and access.

Just about every basement has two key characteristics: masonry walls and floors, and restricted daylight. The type of basement (see below) affects how much difficulty these characteristics impose on a use and design plan, and they affect your choices for finishing surfaces. Start by considering your type of basement, then evaluate your options:

Standard

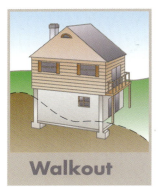

Walkout

Standard Basement

The standard basement is completely surrounded by subterranean foundation walls, with just a bit—maybe 20 percent—above grade. Sometimes small windows peek out from the tops of the walls. Access and egress are via an interior stairway only. Light is a major concern, along with the coolness of all that concrete and limited air circulation.

Walkout Basement

A sloping grade allows at least one wall to be exposed on a walkout basement. Often, this allows more light to reach the interior, but an overhead deck, small door, or few windows can significantly reduce sunlight. Windows and doors improve air circulation. Access and egress are via both interior stairs and an exterior doorway, making this space usable for bedrooms.

◄ *A walkout basement presents many of the same challenges for finishing as a standard basement, except one: light. This house takes full advantage with large windows and a sliding glass door that opens onto an arbored patio. Indoor and outdoor spaces blend, creating an "extra" room complete with outdoor fireplace.*

Floors

Almost all basement subfloors are concrete slab. You can apply or install many kinds of flooring products over concrete for an attractive, durable finish.

Concrete Care

Most concrete slabs have small cracks and other imperfections. You can install some floor coverings, such as carpeting and laminate plank floors, directly over cracks less than ¼-inch wide. Other materials, such as vinyl sheet flooring, require the subfloor to be free from imperfections. Cracks wider than ¼ inch may indicate foundation problems, so consult a foundation contractor before installing a floor covering.

Level any uneven floors or sloped concrete subfloors with gypsum-based leveling compound. This thick, liquid compound is poured directly onto the floor to a thickness of about ½ inch. When cured, the compound will be smooth and level, and will provide a good base for many types of flooring.

Basement slabs in newly constructed houses require about two years to fully cure and release all their interior moisture. Wait until the slab is cured completely before installing finished flooring.

Remember that concrete slabs are in constant contact with the ground beneath them, so they tend to remain cool. If you plan to spend a lot of time in the basement, choose a floor covering that separates your feet from the chill.

Carpet

Carpet is an excellent basement floor covering. The softness of carpeting provides relief from the hardness of the concrete subfloor, and the look is warm and inviting. Installing carpet over concrete is easy—perimeter tack strips specifically made for concrete hold the carpet in place. If you've solved basement dampness problems, there shouldn't be cause for concern about moisture getting trapped underneath. For an extra measure of protection, seal the concrete with a urethane concrete sealer or concrete paint prior to installing the carpet. Choose a rubber pad—foam pads may deteriorate with prolonged exposure to humid conditions.

Paint

A cost-effective way to finish concrete basement subfloors is to paint them. Paint is an especially good finish for workshops or hobby rooms where frequent cleanup is necessary. Epoxy-based paints are tough, resistant to stains and abrasion, and a good choice for high-traffic areas. But they are difficult to apply. Latex-based masonry paints are easier to apply but aren't as durable. Some paints made for use over concrete and masonry are designed as wall sealants and shouldn't be used for covering floors. Be sure to check labels for the manufacturer's instructions and recommendations.

Before you paint, make sure the concrete is clean and free of surface defects. Fill any cracks and chips with hydraulic cement, then trowel them even with the surrounding surfaces. Occasionally, you'll find that finished concrete has a slightly glossy finish caused by careful smoothing when it was poured. For the best adhesion, etch the floor surface with a liquid de-glosser and allow it to dry thoroughly before applying paint.

▲ *Black-and-white adhesive-backed vinyl tiles provide a classic look for this imaginative '50s reproduction diner recreated in a standard basement. Vinyl tiles are durable and inexpensive and are a good choice for do-it-yourself installations.*

Ceramic Tile

Durable, beautiful, and installed easily over concrete, ceramic tile comes in many styles, colors, and textures. One drawback for ceramic tile installed in a basement is that it tends to stay cool, especially during colder months. An excellent, but expensive, solution is to install a radiant floor heat system. This type of system is "buried" inside a thin gypsum mortar base poured over the existing slab. And, the gypsum forms a smooth, flat surface, the perfect substrate for ceramic tile. In new construction, have your contractor install the system directly in the slab (see page 66).

Although installation of ceramic tile is straightforward, it is a relatively slow process. Expect to pay a premium price for a professional to install a ceramic tile floor, or allow plenty of time to install it yourself.

▲ *This streamlined basement design features an especially durable commercial-grade carpeting over the concrete slab. Near the glass block wall, an insert of contrasting color has been cut into the carpeting in soft curves that echo the rounded forms of the overall design.*

Vinyl

Vinyl sheet goods and vinyl tiles are tough, cost-effective floor coverings. They are easily glued to concrete subfloors. Cushion-backed sheet vinyl offers an extra measure of comfort over hard concrete slabs. For any vinyl product, make sure the subfloor is completely smooth and free of defects prior to installation. Otherwise, imperfections, such as cracks, eventually will show through the flooring and possibly cause the material to tear. Repair cracks and chips with hydraulic cement and trowel the surface smooth.

Although vinyl products are virtually waterproof, persistent moisture may cause discoloration of the flooring. If your basement has moisture problems, it is important that you solve them before installing vinyl flooring.

If your basement has many structural posts or other obstructions, installing sheet goods may be difficult, but you can readily trim vinyl tiles to fit.

Laminate Plank

Plastic laminate plank flooring is made from the same material used to make laminate kitchen countertops. It is extremely durable and resistant to stains, abrasion, and moisture. The planks are usually made to look like wood. They are an attractive alternative to real wood flooring (see below). Because laminate plank flooring sits on a cushioned backing and the tongue-and-groove planks are glued to each other—not directly fastened to the subfloor—this type of flooring is ideal for basement applications. Minor cracks and imperfections in the slab will not affect installation.

Wood

Most wood flooring is not recommended for "below-grade" installations, and most manufacturers include a disclaimer on their packaging. Humid conditions affect the performance of wood placed on basement concrete slabs, causing warping and other defects.

Some wood flooring is made of thin layers of wood veneer glued together, and you can install particular types of this laminated wood flooring on a wooden subfloor over a vapor barrier (see below). Check the manufacturer's recommendations to be sure it will work in your basement.

Installing a Plywood Subfloor

For comfort underfoot or to span an uneven concrete slab, install a wooden subfloor. In a typical installation, 5/8- or 3/4-inch exterior-grade plywood sheets are nailed to a grid of *sleepers*—pressure-treated 2x4s laid flat to help keep the finished height within the 90 inches required by building codes. Correct any unevenness in the concrete with shims placed beneath the sleepers. Fill spaces between the sleepers with rigid foam insulation before nailing the plywood in place. The result is a smooth, even subfloor that will accept most types of flooring.

As an added precaution against moisture penetration, lay sheets of 6 mil polyethylene over the slab under the sleepers.

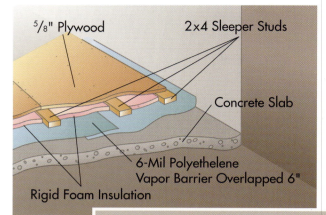

▲ *A wood subfloor installed over a concrete slab starts with a vapor barrier. Then a grid of flat 2x4s is filled with moisture-resistant foam insulation and topped with exterior-grade plywood.*

▲ *Tough epoxy-based paint makes a durable floor covering for a basement workshop. Resistant to stains and chipping, this floor cleans up easily with a broom or damp mop.*

◄ *These 2-foot-square carpet tiles come with adhesive backing for easy installation. Placed directly on a clean, dry concrete slab, they make quick work of carpeting a basement.*

Walls

Foundation walls usually are made of poured concrete or stacked concrete block—not the most attractive surfaces. Fortunately, you often can cover basement walls quickly and inexpensively. Attaching wood furring strips to flat, dry masonry walls, then covering the strips or studs with drywall, gives your walls a smooth, even surface that accepts any type of finish material. You can paint, wallpaper, or tile to complement your decor. Add decorative moldings, such as wainscoting, to increase the appeal of the room.

To make your basement more energy efficient, fill the spaces between the furring strips with rigid insulation. Also, it's easy to install electrical wiring, television cable, speaker wire, and telephone line in this type of wall system.

If basement walls are bowed or out-of-plumb, build a stud wall in front of them to ensure a flat, plumb, finished wall surface. The stud wall is not attached to the masonry wall. Just like a partition wall, the top plate is attached to overhead joists and the bottom plate is nailed to the concrete slab. Insulate with fiberglass batts.

Bowed or out-of-plumb walls may, however, indicate a serious problem that needs to be corrected before the basement is converted to living space. Before proceeding, consult a qualified foundation contractor for a complete evaluation.

Partition Walls

Because partition walls have no structural responsibilities, they are easy to construct and install in virtually any basement location. This versatility makes them ideal for camouflaging posts and other obstructions that can't be moved.

Typical stud wall construction is sufficient for partition walls, but don't rule out flights of fancy. Curved walls or walls made of glass block are simple ways to enhance a basement.

Insulate partition stud walls that define private spaces such as offices or bedrooms with fiberglass batts to reduce sound transmission.

Painting Foundation Walls

Give your basement a low-cost facelift simply by painting masonry foundation walls. Keep in mind that paint won't hide such defects as cracks, chips, holes, and missing mortar. Even if defects are patched, the repairs may appear through the paint.

For the best results, prepare wall surfaces thoroughly, applying paint only to surfaces that are free of dirt, dust, and grease. It is especially important to correct any moisture problems and allow wall surfaces to dry before painting.

Prepare the walls using a wire brush to remove loose dirt and old mortar. Check walls for efflorescence—a white, powdery deposit that sometimes appears on concrete or concrete block walls. Efflorescence is caused by salts in the concrete that, over time, make their way to the surface. Although efflorescent deposits are harmless, remove them before walls are painted. Use soap and water and a stiff brush to scrub off the deposits. Be sure to rinse thoroughly with water and allow the walls to dry completely. If efflorescence remains, scrub the walls with a solution of 1 part muriatic acid to 20 parts water to help remove the deposits.

Paint prepared walls with a good quality latex paint. Be sure to read the manufacturer's recommendations about painting basement walls. During the painting process, have a portable dehumidifier running to keep humidity levels low and to help the paint dry completely.

Some types of paint are made specifically to seal walls against moisture. Called "waterproofing paint" or "masonry waterproofers," these tough coatings contain mixtures of synthetic rubber and portland cement. They are designed to seal the pores of cement and cement block, reducing the penetration of moisture due to capillary action. Although not a true waterproofing system, this kind of paint can stand up to the kinds of moisture that would cause regular latex paints to blister and peel. It is available in standard colors or can be tinted to a desired color.

Brick or Stone Veneers

An alternative to traditional finishes, such as paint and wallpaper, is a masonry veneer. The look is especially handsome in basements, where you can make your walls look like antique rustic foundations. Condensation and other minor moisture problems will not affect masonry veneer walls.

You can apply masonry veneer directly to unpainted, untreated concrete or concrete block walls. If the walls have been painted or treated

Walls needn't be only straight and flat. Here, a short, irregular stud wall has been added to give three-dimensional shape and add architectural interest to an ordinary basement wall. The light and shadow created by adjustable ceiling-mounted spotlights, lighted pedestals, and floor lamps banish any hint of boxiness.

A brick veneer gives this basement room a rustic elegance. The veneer is installed over plywood attached to the concrete foundation walls. This application works especially well because it makes an attractive, fireproof backing for the wood-burning stove.

with a sealant, you'll need to install furring strips covered with sheets of plywood to create a backing for the veneer. For brick veneers, nail a plastic form to the plywood to align the bricks. For setting rough stone, apply a wire mesh to the plywood backing to help hold a base coat of mortar.

Solid stone and brick are heavy materials and may require additional support. Typically, you must install a new foundation footing. In a retrofit situation, this means removing a portion of the existing slab to pour a new footing—a messy and expensive job.

Cast stone products, made to imitate many types of stone and brick, are thinner and weigh less than real masonry, cost less, and install faster. Unlike real stone, they require no additional foundation support.

Ceramic Tile

Tile is an elegant material that can greatly improve the look of any room, but consider carefully before installing tile on foundation walls. These walls have a tendency to move slightly over time—movement that may crack the tiles or fracture grout lines. Tile is also a relatively expensive finish material. You'll want surrounding surfaces to be in keeping with the look of tile.

You can apply ceramic tile directly to masonry foundation walls as long as these walls are smooth and dry. Installation is less successful directly over concrete block because the surface is uneven. In this case, first cover the masonry wall with cement-like *backer board* before installing tile. This will achieve the required smooth, even surface. Backer board is ½-inch-thick sheet material made specifically for tile installations.

▲ *This simple but attractive wall treatment starts with drywall applied to furring strips, creating a smooth, even wall surface—the perfect base for wallpaper and wainscoting. The strong vertical lines of the wallpaper help visually raise the height of the room.*

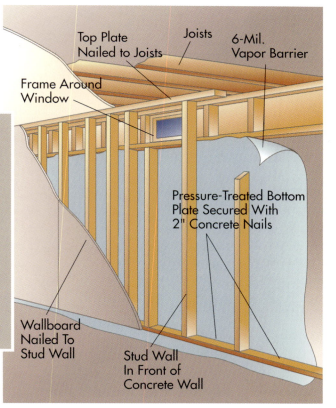

▲ Basement walls don't have to be static. This lower level exercise room features a curved partition wall with a painted drywall finish and a wall made of glass block. Glass block allows light to shine through, an important consideration for basement locations.

➤ Drywall installs easily over non-bearing stud walls set in front of the foundation wall. A full stud wall allows accessible space for electrical wiring, telephone lines, and television cables. Fill the cavities between the studs with fiberglass batts.

Top Plate Nailed to Joists

Joists

6-Mil. Vapor Barrier

Frame Around Window

Pressure-Treated Bottom Plate Secured With 2" Concrete Nails

Wallboard Nailed To Stud Wall

Stud Wall In Front of Concrete Wall

Ceilings

Basement ceilings are difficult to finish because often there is an array of obstructions, such as pipes, ducts, and wires, all attached to the underside of the overhead joists or running between them. You usually can move wires and water supply pipes, but finding acceptable new routes for ductwork or drain lines often is difficult. One option is to disguise or box-in obstructions within a wood framework, then cover the frame with finish materials.

The three primary options for finishing basement ceilings are painting, installing a suspended ceiling, or covering the joists with drywall or wood. Another possibility is attaching fabric panels to joists and letting the fabric hang slightly for a billowing effect. You must install certain flammable materials, such as mirrored acrylic panels or wood, over a layer of drywall to meet building code fire safety requirements.

Painting

One low-cost finishing option is to leave all the elements in the ceiling exposed but camouflage the overhead tangle with a coat of paint. Painting everything a single color makes the different elements blend together, an they become less noticeable. A paint sprayer will coat everything evenly—including the sides and much of the upper surfaces of various elements. Paint the joists, the underside of the subfloor, wires, pipes, and ducts. Both light and dark colors work well. Dark colors disguise the many elements better, while light colors help make the space brighter. To complete the camouflage, paint the walls a different color.

Suspended Ceilings

A low-cost, low-maintenance option is to install a drop or suspended ceiling system. This system includes a framework of metal channels hung on wires attached to the joists. The channels support lightweight acoustical panels that form a uniform, finished surface. The system has several advantages for basement applications. Moving wires, pipes, or ducts is unnecessary, and joists do not have to be straight for the finished ceiling to be flat and level. Accessing heating, cooling, or electrical systems is a simple matter of temporarily removing a panel. You can add lighting by removing an acoustical panel and fitting the opening with a drop-in fixture made

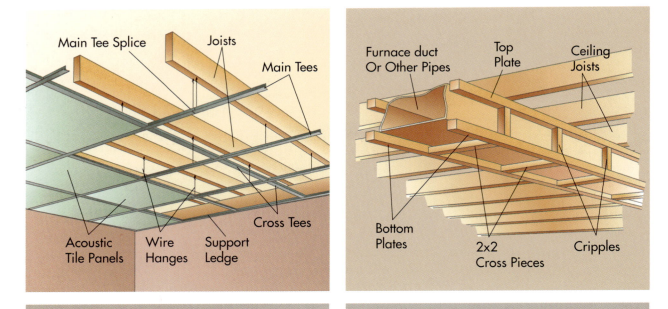

▲ *A suspended ceiling is installed underneath the overhead floor joists. A grid of metal channels is hung from the joists, then acoustical panels are placed in the grid. Suspended ceilings hide pipes and wires and present a smooth, even surface.*

▲ *Ductwork usually cannot be moved, so it must be hidden. One method is to frame the outside of the duct with 2x2-inch strips of wood. The framework is not attached to the duct. Rather, it is nailed together and attached to overhead joists.*

specifically for the purpose. Suspended ceilings have the added benefit of insulating unwanted noise from upstairs rooms.

You'll need adequate headroom to install a suspended ceiling. Building codes generally specify at least 90 inches (7 feet, 6 inches) of headroom from finished floor to finished ceiling in main living areas. Also, 90 inches from the floor is the minimum distance allowed for a ceiling lighting fixture.

Suspended ceiling systems offer many styles of channels and decorative panels. If you're considering a suspended ceiling, check supplier's catalogues and home improvement centers to find a style that fits your plans.

Installing Drywall

Drywall on ceilings creates a smooth, even finish and helps give a basement the sense of being part of the main living area. It's an excellent base for paint and other materials, such as wood paneling and reflective acrylic sheets. For safety, building codes typically require that you install flammable materials, such as wood paneling, only over drywall because of its fire-retardant quality.

Before installing drywall, clear all obstructions. Relocate pipes and wires so they are not in the way.

▲ *This stylish suspended ceiling system features textured acoustical panels and fluorescent lighting fixtures designed to fit into the grid pattern. Acoustical panels help reduce noise from this teenager's game room.*

New holes can be drilled in the joists to accommodate relocated elements, but there are restrictions to ensure the joists maintain structural integrity:

■ Holes cannot be larger than one-fourth the depth of the joist.

■ Holes must be spaced at least 6 inches apart.

■ Holes are permitted only when joists are larger than 2x6.

Consult a qualified building or remodeling contractor if you have concerns about moving obstructions in your basement ceiling.

Box in large obstructions, such as ducts and drain pipes, with a wooden framework. Cover this with drywall or other finish materials (see page 46). Although such obstructions often are unavoidable, careful planning will ensure that any boxed-in elements become an integral part of your basement design scheme.

Joists must be straight and their bottom edges in line with one another to provide an even surface for the drywall. To determine if joists are straight, stand on a ladder and sight along the bottoms of the joists.

Severely sagging or bowed joists need to be straightened before installing drywall. Typically, a hydraulic floor jack and a post are used to return the joists to level. Then they are strengthened by installing another joist alongside and bolting the two joists together. This technique, called *sistering,* requires that the ends of new joists rest on foundation walls or other load-bearing support walls. If sagging is slight, shims can provide a level surface.

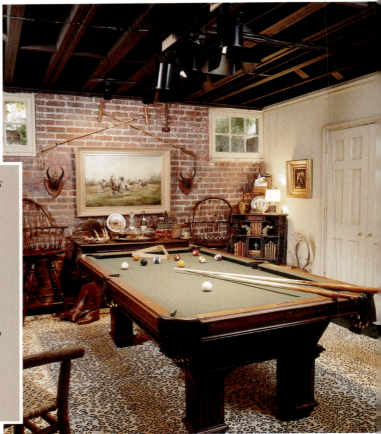

▶ *The fact that this basement ceiling has been left uncovered doesn't detract from the comfortable interior design and furnishings. A dark stain unites the ceiling elements into a single block of color that helps disguise imperfections.*

▶ *To see if overhead joists are sagging, stand on a ladder and sight along the joist bottoms. You'll quickly determine if the surfaces are even enough to accept drywall. If joists are cracked or sagging, consult a building contractor about strengthening them.*

Mirrored Ceilings

Because the ceilings typically are low, highly reflective finish materials, such as mirrored acrylic sheets, can help make basement rooms appear more spacious. Some suspended roof systems offer custom reflective panels that install easily in the grid. Or, you can purchase reflective acrylic sheets to cover a drywall ceiling. Expect to pay between $125 and $175 for a ⅛-inch-thick, 4x8-foot sheet of mirrored acrylic. Installation includes mechanical fasteners, such as screws or bolts, to attach the sheets to joists. Don't rely on construction adhesive alone to do the job. Some adhesives react with acrylic and can fail to hold the panel in place.

Sound Insulation

To deaden the sound of footsteps and other noises from rooms overhead, install fiberglass batt insula-

▲ *Even though this basement has a low ceiling, it seems spacious, thanks to acrylic mirrored panels attached to the ceiling. The highly reflective panels not only give the illusion of volume, but they also reflect ambient light and help brighten the room.*

tion between the overhead floor joists. Also add sound insulation for bedrooms, offices, and other areas where noise might be a distraction, or to muffle noise from a basement activity room where televisions and stereos are located. Used in combination with acoustical ceiling tiles, fiberglass insulation significantly reduces sound transmission.

You can cut and shape fiberglass batts to fit around pipes, ducts, and other obstructions. To make installation easy, place the facing on the bottom side and use the edges of the facing for stapling the batts into position.

Windows and Doors

Opening up the space to daylight is one of the best ways to make a basement more livable. For a standard, below-grade basement, you can install either new larger windows, or additional small windows, to greatly increase the amount of daylight entering the space. Gaining direct access to the basement from the outside greatly improves the usability of the space. For standard basements, bulkhead access doors provide a convenient way to move furniture, workshop supplies, or other large items in and out of the basement.

Adding Windows

Before installing new windows in your basement, evaluate the condition of the foundation, check the location of floor joists and other structural elements, and examine the area immediately outside the proposed window location. If you are adding a bedroom, you'll need to provide an egress opening (see information at right). Consult a building or remodeling contractor to help you determine the feasibility of installing new windows.

Install basement windows on the south-facing side of the house to gather maximum sunlight during winter months. Consider privacy, too. Avoid placing windows close to sidewalks or houses. Use fences, walls, and plantings to maintain privacy.

Adding or enlarging basement windows is not a job for the average do-it-yourselfer. It involves removing portions of the foundation wall, and supporting the structure above the wall opening with a header designed to span the opening and carry the weight of the house. Cutting concrete or concrete block and maintaining structural integrity are tasks best left to an experienced professional.

According to building codes, the outside bottom edge of the new window should be at least 6 inches above the soil, to prevent leakage from ground water and to keep wood framing members from rotting. The space between the bottom of the header and a point 6 inches above the soil line should be big enough to install a window unit at least 1 foot high.

Window openings that extend below grade must have a window well. Installing a window well requires excavating the soil outside foundation walls and putting in a retaining wall of galvanized steel or masonry. The floor of the well must have a drainage system, preferably a gravel bed and a drain pipe connected to a perimeter drain (see page 53). If there is no perimeter drain, the gravel bed must be about 6 inches deep to hold precipitation until it percolates into the surrounding soil. Install rigid foam insulation between the gravel bed and the foundation to encourage water to migrate away from the wall.

You can cover window wells with a translucent covering, much like a skylight. The covering prevents precipitation and debris from entering the area. Either hinge coverings to allow air circulation, or fix them in place and seal them against moisture.

▲ *This basement bedroom conforms to building codes by including an egress window. Here, the space necessary for climbing out of the basement is provided by a prefabricated well made of high-density polyethylene. The built-in steps can be used for potted plants. (From Bilco Co.)*

Egress Windows

Basement bedrooms must have an exit, usually a window for standard basements, with an opening no less than 5 square feet and a minimum width of 24 inches. This window, called an egress window, allows a person to escape in an emergency. For

▲ The owners of this suburban house took advantage of a generous amount of above-grade wall area by bumping out the wall to create a basement sunroom. The bottoms of the windows are just above soil level. This south-facing arrangement gathers plenty of winter sunshine.

access to the window opening, locate it no more than 42 inches from the floor. Installing an egress window is possible only if you have the space outside your home to accommodate a large window well, one spacious enough to permit a person to enter the well from inside the home and then exit the well safely. For this reason, egress wells often feature a stairway or permanent ladder.

There's no need for the area outside an egress window to be stark. Style an egress window with potted plants and other items to create an attractive window garden. Prefabricated egress wells made of fiberglass include stepped sides to assist in exiting the house. The steps make good shelves for compact plants.

Bulkhead Access Doors

Installing a bulkhead access door can be expensive and will probably require the services of a contractor, but the convenience and accessibility it provides may be worth the investment. For installation,

▲ *This small basement window has illusions of grandeur. Casement molding that extends below the window and closed cafe shutters give the illusion of a much larger opening.*

▲ *Bulkhead doors make basements readily accessible from the outside. They are especially helpful for accessing basement workshops, and for moving large items, such as patio furniture, in and out of seasonal storage. (From Bilco Co.)*

excavate a hole large enough to accommodate a stairway, about 8x8 feet, next to the foundation. Reinforce the sides of the excavation with masonry, and cut a doorway into the existing foundation. Once the sidewalls are complete, install insulated double doors over the opening. Bulkhead doors are typically made of reinforced steel and are locked from the inside.

As a final step, install exterior-type passage doors in the foundation opening. For an extra measure of security, install locks in these doors.

Bulkhead doors also are available as prefabricated units, complete with poured concrete steps. The units also include side walls and doors. A crane is needed to lift these units into place. It usually takes about a day to install them, including excavation. To locate a professional who installs bulkhead doors, ask a building contractor or look in the Yellow Pages of your telephone directory under "Excavating Contractors" and "Foundation Contractors."

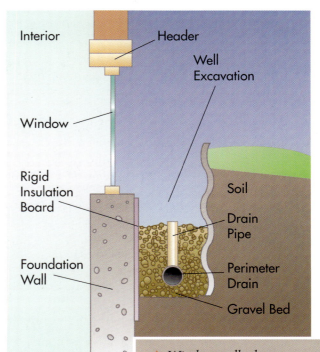

▲ *Window wells that are open to the elements should include a drain for carrying away accumulated precipitation. Ideally, the system would include a 6-inch-deep gravel drain bed and a 1-inch drain pipe connected to a perimeter drain system.*

■ *Installing a window well made of galvanized steel is not difficult. The well should be at least 8 inches wider than the window opening and extend at least 12 inches below the level of the windowsill. The soil around the window opening should be removed to a depth equal to the depth of the well. The well is attached to the foundation walls with masonry anchors, then filled with 6 inches of gravel.*

Keeping Basements **Dry**

Eliminating moisture-related problems is the first step in converting an unused basement into a living area.

If your basement is five years old or older, stays dry during rainy seasons, and shows no obvious signs of water damage, such as staining, chances are it will continue to remain dry. Keeping up with maintenance to prevent water from collecting near the foundation helps ensure freedom from moisture-related problems.

Obvious water problems, such as puddles, "weeping" walls, or periodic flooding, require corrective measures. With the exception of routine maintenance, most basement waterproofing is done from the inside; only extremely wet conditions require a costly excavation on the exterior side of foundation walls in order to apply waterproofing materials and install drainage systems.

Even if you have no immediate plans for converting basement space to living area, it is still worth the effort and expense to correct moisture problems. Real estate agents estimate that an obviously wet basement can reduce the resale value of a home by 10 to 20 percent.

New homes under construction should have exterior basement walls "damp-proofed" or waterproofed when the foundation is exposed prior to backfilling (see "Damp-Proofing and Waterproofing New Homes," page 63).

◄ The most reliable waterproofing system includes a drain screen—sheets of rigid fiberglass or extruded polystyrene—that are installed against basement walls. The screen interrupts hydrostatic pressure and allows water to fall to a perimeter drain. The screen also prevents the inner asphalt coating from being damaged during backfilling. (From Koch Waterproofing Solutions)

Testing for Moisture

Perform a simple test to help you determine the sources of moisture infiltrating your basement. Tape large squares of aluminum foil (1-foot square or larger) at various locations on the walls and floors of the basement. Use duct tape to completely seal all edges. Leave the aluminum foil in place for several days. If droplets form on the undersides of the foil, moisture is migrating through the masonry. See page 60 for solutions. If droplets form on top of the foil, then the basement has high humidity, and condensation is the likely problem.

Humid Air and Condensation

Basements are constantly under attack from many naturally occurring sources of moisture. The most common is humid air condensing on walls or exposed pipes. Uncorrected, condensation can blister painted surfaces, cause stains, and "weep" onto floors, creating puddles. The problem is especially acute during rainy seasons when windows and doors remain partially open and humid air enters the house. This air, laden with moisture, is heavy. Gravity tends to pull heavy air down into basement rooms, where it condenses as it comes into contact with cool surfaces. The problem is usually not as noticeable during the summer when windows and doors are closed and the air-conditioning system is running. Air conditioning helps remove moisture from interior air. In the winter, air is naturally drier and less likely to produce condensation.

▲ *To test your basement for moisture problems, use duct tape to fasten squares of aluminum foil to walls and floors. Completely seal the edges of the foil with the tape. Droplets forming on the undersides indicate moisture is penetrating the masonry from outside. Droplets on top indicate condensation from humid air.*

Check for Leaks

Sometimes, what appears to be condensation on pipes is actually water from leaks. Before taking corrective measures for excess humidity, check pipe joints and fittings for leaks. Wipe away water droplets hanging from pipes. If the droplets reappear within a few moments, there may be a leak. Have a qualified plumber make the necessary repairs.

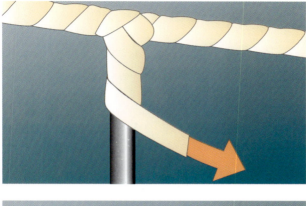

▲ *Covering exposed water supply pipes prevents humid air from condensing on pipe surfaces. Both insulating tape* (top) *and foam sleeve insulation* (bottom) *are made specifically for pipes.*

Fixing Condensation Problems

Proper ventilation is the best solution for reducing condensation. Open basement windows during good weather to encourage air circulation.

Another way to prevent condensation is to prevent moist air from coming in contact with cool basement surfaces. Cover exposed pipes with adhesive-backed insulating tape or foam sleeve insulation. These materials are made specifically for pipes, install easily, and are available at home improvement centers and hardware stores.

Remove excess humidity in the basement with a portable dehumidifier. These units are compact, run off regular household current, and can be purchased for $100 to $250. They are rated according to their capacity, usually 25, 40, or 50 pints (see chart below). For top efficiency, close doors and windows to make sure fresh, humid air doesn't continually flowing into the basement while your dehumidifier is running.

Damp walls can result from humid air coming in contact with cool concrete surfaces. Walls that are covered with framing materials and rigid foam are insulated from contact with humid air (see "Walls," pages 42–45).

How to Choose a Dehumidifier

Use the chart as a guideline for room size. You can get exact square footage by multiplying the length and width of your room.

Compare approximate room sizes listed at the top of the chart to the level of humidity in the room. That determines dehumidifier capacity required.

Humidity Level	Capacity (in pints) Required (by area of room)				
	500 s.f.	1000 s.f.	1500 s.f.	2000 s.f.	2500 s.f.
Moderately Damp: *Room feels damp and has musty odor only in humid weather.*	25	25	25	25	40
Very Damp: *Room always feels damp and has musty odor. Damp spots show on walls or floors.*	25	25	25	40	40
Wet Room: *Room feels damp and smells wet. Wall or floor seepage is present most of the time.*	25	25	40	40	50
Extremely Wet: *Room is used for laundry drying. Wall or floor seepage is always present.*	25	40	40	50	50

Hydrostatic Pressure and Capillary Action

When your house was built, earth was removed to make way for constructing the foundation walls. Once the foundation was completed, some of that soil was replaced. This process, known as backfilling, puts loose soil around the foundation. This soil soaks up water like a sponge. Water-soaked soil puts pressure against the foundation walls, causing uneven settling, and leaky basements. This pressure is called *hydrostatic pressure*.

The condition worsens as backfilled soil compacts over time, creating low spots that trap rainwater and increasing the moisture content of the soil next to the foundation.

The pressure of water-soaked soil also cracks basement walls. The damage usually occurs during colder months, when water-laden soil freezes and expands, pushing against basement walls with enough force to crack the masonry. Small cracks don't jeopardize the integrity of the foundation, but they do provide water with an easy path to the interior of your home. If the pressure has been great enough to bow your basement walls, seek the advice of a professional concrete or basement contractor. Bowed walls may need to be braced.

The porosity of basement walls is another concern. Even though walls made of concrete or cement block seem completely solid, they contain many tiny imperfections or pores. These pores are conduits for moisture, channeling water toward the interior in a process known as capillary action.

This condition usually is worse during summer months. When windows are open, warm air flows toward the upper levels of a house, pulling air from the lower areas. This natural air flow can create a slightly negative atmospheric pressure in the basement, drawing moisture into the basement through the pores in basement walls.

For these reasons it is important to schedule periodic inspections and maintenance of your home's exterior. Keeping excess moisture out of the soil surrounding your home will relieve hydrostatic pressure against basement walls and reduce moisture brought to interiors by capillary action.

Preventive Maintenance to Reduce Hydrostatic Pressure

The most common cause of basement moisture problems comes from excess rainwater and melted snow that gathers in the soil surrounding a home's foundation. A heavy, 1-inch rain shower would pour almost 1,000 gallons of water on a 1,600-square-foot roof. All that water is shed by the roof into a home's system of gutters and downspouts, and ends up on the ground near foundation walls.

You can help reduce the chance of problems by making sure this water flows away from your foundation and the backfill soil that surrounds foundation walls. Grade the soil around the foundation so it slopes away from the house at a rate of about 2

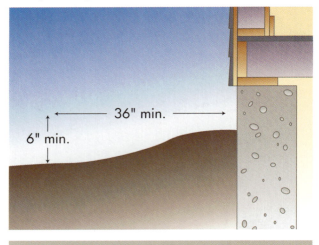

▲ *Ensuring proper grading of soils next to foundation walls is one of the best ways to prevent moisture damage to basement interiors. Check to make sure soil slopes 6 vertical inches for a distance of 3 horizontal feet.*

vertical inches for every horizontal foot over a distance of at least 3 feet. This ensures most water ends up beyond the porous backfill soil. Fill low spots with dirt—not rock or gravel—for proper drainage.

Debris collecting inside the gutters can dam downspouts, causing water to overflow and end up next to the foundation. Clean them in the spring and fall to avoid problems. Make sure all gutters are straight and slope gently toward downspout

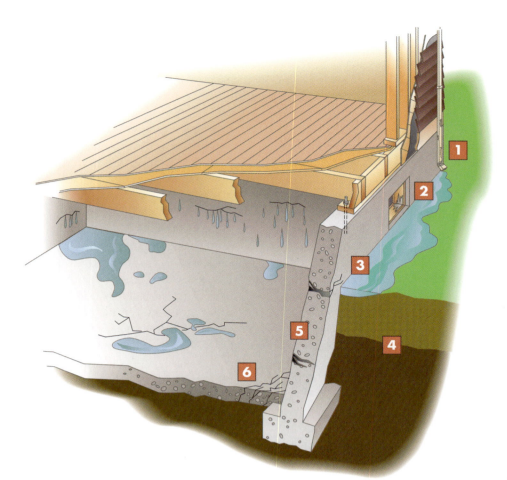

◀ *A variety of problems can cause basement leaks and other moisture problems:*
1) downspouts too short
2) windows set too close to grade
3) inadequate grading of soils near foundation walls
4) high water table
5) cracked walls
6) floor slab cracked by hydrostatic pressure

▶ *Solutions for moisture problems:*
1) adding splash blocks or extending downspouts
2) installing window wells
3) adding soil to achieve proper grade slope
4) installing a perimeter drain system to carry away excess water
5) coating interior walls and floors with waterproofing paint

locations. Sagging gutters trap water in low spots and cause overflowing. Downspouts should extend at least 5 feet from foundation walls. Lengthen short downspouts or place concrete splash blocks beneath downspout openings to direct water away from foundation walls.

Sealing Interior Walls

Several products are available that coat interior walls and stop capillary action, thus preventing moisture from migrating through foundation walls. Before these products are applied, thoroughly scrub walls clean, and seal cracks and other holes with hydraulic cement or silicone caulk. You can apply hydraulic cement even when cracks are leaking actively. Silicone caulk works best when applied to thin cracks that are free from moisture.

■ Waterproofing paints, properly applied over a clean surface, can do an adequate job of preventing moisture migration due to capillary action. Latex waterproofing paints have low odor—a consideration in basements with limited ventilation—but are somewhat less effective than oil-based waterproofing paints. These paints can help stop moisture migration but should not be considered a foolproof waterproofing measure.

■ Cement-based waterproofing coatings adhere well to masonry surfaces and often are used to seal swimming pools. These thick coatings leave a somewhat rough-finished texture, but do an exceptional job of stopping moisture.

■ Epoxy-based coatings are exceptionally durable. They are also expensive. Mix these two-part coatings before application. And be sure to allow for adequate ventilation—it's essential when working with epoxy compounds.

The Test of Time

Controlling condensation, carrying out exterior drainage maintenance, and sealing interior walls may solve basement moisture problems immediately but can fail over time. Wait one year to gauge the effectiveness of the techniques described above.

If excessive moisture remains a problem, consult a remodeling contractor or professional basement contractor. You may need to install an interior drainage system, or you may have to excavate basement walls to apply exterior waterproofing.

High Water Table

Occasionally, a house is constructed in an area with a high water table—naturally occurring water that flows through soil like an underground river. With changing seasons, water tables fluctuate. When they are low, a basement appears dry and free from problems. When water tables rise, they can engulf a foundation and cause basement flooding. A house can be built when water tables were low and no problems were apparent only to develop problems later as the water table rises. The best remedy is to install an interior drain system and a sump pump (see page 62). A high water table can be a persistent problem with no foolproof solution. Houses should not be built on sites with known high water tables.

Interior Drainage Systems

Interior drainage systems are also called de-watering systems. This means that water cannot be stopped from entering the home but is intercepted where the foundation walls meet the floor. From that point, water is directed to a sump pump so it can be removed. Expect to pay between $1,000 and $2,500 for an interior drainage system.

There are two types of de-watering systems. One requires a 1-foot-wide channel cut in the perimeter of your basement floor, all the way through the concrete. Perforated plastic drain pipe is fitted into the channel and covered with gravel. New concrete is then poured over the gravel to floor level. A slight space is left between the floor and the wall to allow weeping walls to drain directly into the channel. The drain pipe leads to a reservoir equipped with a sump pump. Excess water drains into the reservoir and is drawn outside the house by the sump pump. Although the excavation process is noisy and messy—it requires the use of a jackhammer to break the concrete—the job usually takes only a day or two to complete. Because this de-watering system is installed below the level of the floor, it is sometimes effective in preventing problems caused by rising water tables.

The second type of de-watering system does not open up the basement floor. Instead, plastic channels are fixed to the basement walls with waterproof glue where the walls meet the floor, much like baseboard trim. The channels direct excess water to a sump pump location. The method is not

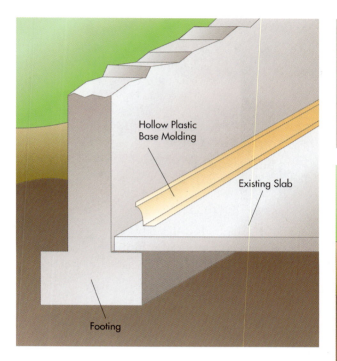

Hollow Plastic
Base Molding

Existing Slab

Footing

▲ *An interior drainage system is installed along the perimeter of the basement slab. Here, a hollow plastic molding is glued to the wall, trapping water and channeling it to a sump pump for removal.*

▼ *To install this interior drainage system along the perimeter of the basement slab, a portion of the slab is removed and a trench dug next to the foundation footing. The trench is filled with drainage gravel and a drain pipe. Water from the pipe is channeled to a sump pump. After installation, the slab is repaired.*

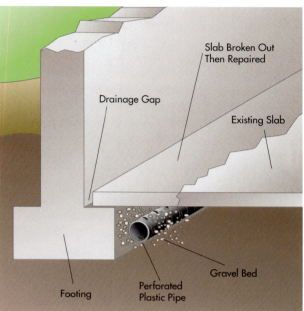

Slab Broken Out
Then Repaired

Drainage Gap

Existing Slab

Footing

Perforated
Plastic Pipe

Gravel Bed

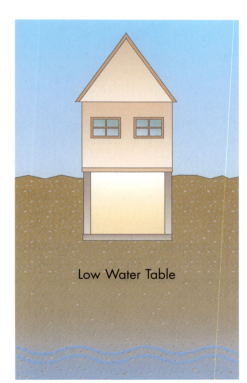

Low Water Table

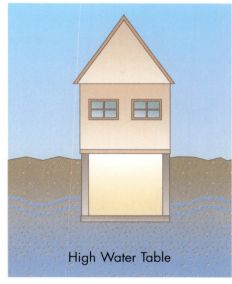

High Water Table

◄ *Seasonal differences in naturally occurring groundwater tables make them difficult to predict. When the table is low (far left), the basement is dry. When tables rise (right), moisture can enter a basement from several locations. A perimeter drain system can help solve problems caused by a high water table.*

Sump Pumps

A sump pump sits in a reservoir below the level of your basement floor. There are two types. A pedestal-type pump has a motor that sits on top of a long pipe. The pipe extends to a base in the bottom of the sump pit. When water enters the pit, it moves a float that engages the motor. Water is then pumped from the pit. A submersible sump pump sits entirely inside the pit. A float attached to the pump signals the motor to switch on, removing the water. A submersible sump pump is considered the more reliable and effective unit.

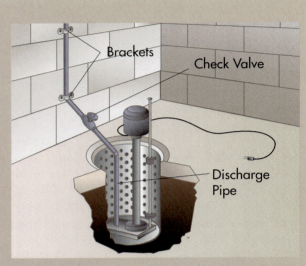

Brackets

Check Valve

Discharge Pipe

Both pumps remove water through a discharge pipe to the outside of the house. The exit location should be treated like a downspout, with proper grading of surrounding soil to drain water away from foundation walls.

One concern about sump pumps is that when they are needed most, for example—during a heavy thunderstorm—is exactly the time when electrical power may be lost. For this reason, consider installing a battery-operated backup system for your pump. In the event electrical power fails, the battery takes over, running the pump for several hours. Expect to pay $1,000 for a top-quality sump pump equipped with a battery backup.

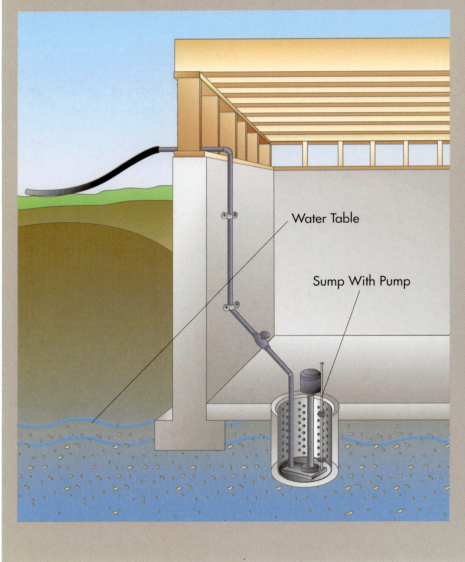

Water Table

Sump With Pump

as effective at intercepting rising water tables as the below-floor system.

Damp-Proofing and Waterproofing New Homes

On most new homes, building contractors damp-proof the exterior side of basement walls prior to backfilling. While effective in preventing capillary action and most types of moisture infiltration, damp-proofing techniques will not stop water under heavy hydrostatic pressure from entering basement walls. Although imperfect, damp-proofing is still beneficial. Before construction begins, make sure your contractor plans to damp-proof your basement walls. If other houses in the area are affected by chronic water problems, you may want to consider an exterior waterproofing system.

Damp-proofing consists of cleaning walls thoroughly and leveling the wall surfaces by *parging*. This involves troweling on a ½-inch-thick coating of cement plaster to the walls. Parging helps seal walls against moisture, but for best results it should be covered with a coating of asphalt or coal-tar pitch. Asphalt emulsions are brushed or troweled on and are the most cost-effective coating available. Hot tar usually is applied over layers of overlapping felt paper, and provides a thicker membrane than asphalt.

Polyethylene sheeting that is manufactured specifically for basement walls is another low-cost option and is sold under many brand names. The sheets are hung from the top of the foundation and draped across the footings. Care must be taken during backfilling not to tear or puncture the sheets.

A waterproofing contractor can install a full waterproofing system. The system, sometimes called a drain screen, includes rigid sheets of waterproof fiberglass or extruded polystyrene attached to the exterior side of the basement walls over a damp-proof coating. These rigid sheets are made of porous materials or with vertical channels that direct groundwater to a gravel bed and drain pipe installed just outside the footing. This system interrupts hydrostatic pressure and allows gravity to draw water down to the perimeter drain pipe and away from the house.

▲ *A full waterproofing system is being installed on the exterior basement walls of this house under construction. The waterproofing contractor, in the foreground, is spraying the foundation walls with an asphalt coating while another worker installs rigid drain screen sheets. (From Koch Waterproofing Solutions)*

Excavating Foundation Walls

Many older homes did not have damp-proofing installed at the time of construction. In severe cases of basement flooding, excavating exterior walls and installing damp-proofing or a full waterproofing system may be required to keep a basement dry. While applying a system to the exterior of the home is an excellent way to prevent further water infiltration, the cost of excavating and installing preventive measures can run between $3,500 and $10,000 or more. The final cost usually is higher because excavating equipment ruins portions of the yard. Trees, bushes, shrubs, and flowers near the perimeter of the house may have to be removed and replanted or, in many cases, are unavoidably destroyed. Ancillary structures, such as decks or porch additions, may have to be altered or torn down. Underground plumbing, cable, telephone, and electrical services may need to be disconnected and then restored—all at additional cost.

Elements of **Style**

Plan for the systems and design elements that will make basement rooms comfortable and beautiful.

Basements are a bit different than other areas of your home. And, while certain elements, such as bathrooms and fireplaces, make wonderful additions to the space, careful planning is required to ensure these elements are installed cost-effectively and function properly. Adaptations can be made, and often the best placement is affected by existing plumbing, wiring, and such.

To keep planning and construction processes on track, have a good understanding of the mechanical systems that affect your basement. Then you can make the best choices about what elements make a basement space comfortable and inviting and how to include them. You also need to be familiar with building codes and the various restrictions and requirements that help make basement rooms safe. It's a good idea to consult an architect, interior designer, or building professional to help you make informed decisions and to keep you aware of building codes (see page 79, "Working With a Design Professional").

▲ With planning, this family accommodated each member's needs in a multipurpose basement room. Recessed lighting, a mini-kitchen, and durable vinyl flooring make the space ideal for familial or social gatherings.

▶ Undeterred by posts and prominent support beams, the owners of this suburban house planned a basement scheme that incorporated the structural elements as an integral part of the interior design. They devoted space behind the posts to generous bookshelf storage and a television cabinet.

Quick-Reference Table of Contents

▼ *The homeowners carefully considered every element of this basement design. Because this room is narrow, they tucked the television and stereo under the stairs. A gas fireplace at one end made the family room especially inviting.*

Heating & Cooling

Critical to making your new living space comfortable, heating and cooling systems deserve time and attention at the beginning of your project. And insulation (see pages 38–49), a key to energy efficiency and maintaining temperature, goes hand-in-hand with heating and cooling.

Heating Options

Heating a basement is a necessity. In many homes with forced-air systems, additional vents can be added to ducts. Consult with a heating and cooling expert for advice about your particular needs.

For extra heating power, you can install an electric baseboard or fan-type electric heater. Built-in thermostats keep temperatures constant. Some models draw a significant amount of electricity, so make sure that the electrical service panel can handle the additional load. A supplemental heating system might require the installation of a separate circuit.

Radiant floor heat is an excellent option for basements. With a radiant heat system, a network of low-voltage electrical cables or flexible hot water tubes are imbedded in the concrete slab. For retrofitting, the system is installed in a bed of lightweight gypsum concrete. Heat radiates from the wires or tubes and warms the surrounding surfaces, creating a dry, even heat. The system is especially compatible with unfinished or painted slabs, or slabs covered with ceramic tile. Other finish materials, such as carpet or laminate flooring, insulate against the heat source, reducing efficiency. Discuss your plans with a professional heating and cooling contractor who specializes in radiant heat systems.

Fireplaces and free-standing stoves are another source of supplemental heat for basement rooms. (see "Fireplaces," pages 74–75).

Cool Choices

For the most part, cooling a standard basement isn't a problem. Surrounded by earth that tends to remain a constant 55° F, a standard basement stays cool even during summer's hottest days. In addition, cool air inside a house collects in the lowest

▲ *This basement features forced air heating and cooling ducts that have been boxed in and covered with drywall (see "Ceilings," page 46).*

level—the basement—making supplemental cooling almost unnecessary.

Walkout basements, however, may require supplemental cooling. Basement doors and windows left uncovered or open on hot summer days can quickly make a cool lower-level refuge uncomfortably warm. If your house has a forced-air heating and cooling system, you may be able to add vent openings in the ducts. Check with a heating and cooling contractor to find out if your furnace and air-conditioning systems can handle the additional load. An alternative is to add a small supplemental unit such as a window air conditioning unit or a ductless air conditioner.

Window air conditioners require a wall opening large enough to accommodate the unit—smaller versions are about 24 inches wide and 16 inches high. The area directly outside the unit must be free of obstructions, such as bushes or shrubs, that might impede air circulation. If you are thinking of putting a window air conditioner in an existing window, remember that you're sacrificing an opening that lets in valuable sunlight.

A better option is a ductless air conditioner. It has an indoor air handler, about 8 inches wide, connected to an outside compressor via refrigerant lines that require only a single 3-inch hole in the wall. The compressor can be located up to 150 feet away from the air handler.

▲ *The architect who designed this stylish basement recreation room was unfazed by the presence of forced air heating and cooling ducts located in the ceiling. He planned an imaginative ceiling design to hide them.*

Bathrooms

Adding a bathroom to your home is a convenience and a good investment. If you decide to sell your home, you are likely to recover about 90 percent of the costs of a bathroom addition.

As it generally isn't the main bathroom for the house, a basement bathroom doesn't have to be large. A space 30 inches wide and 75 inches long—about 16 square feet—is adequate for a toilet and a sink. To include a shower or bathtub, you'll need a space about 5 feet wide and 7 feet long—about 35 square feet. Building codes allow ceiling heights of 84 inches for bathrooms—6 inches lower than for other living areas. This can be an important factor in basements where ceiling height may be restricted by pipes or ductwork.

Getting hot and cold water to the space is usually a simple matter of splicing into existing supply lines. Getting wastewater out can be trickier. The most critical factor in installing a basement bathroom is locating drains and vent stacks. All bathroom fixtures must drain into the main drain line—usually a 3- or 4-inch diameter pipe that enters the basement through the floor above and exits the basement through a wall or the floor. Accessing the main drain for a new basement toilet or shower may mean cutting through a concrete floor. Also, the distance that new fixtures can be located away from the existing drain line is limited—extensions to the line must slope down at the rate of at least 1/4 inch per foot.

If you are considering adding a new bathroom to your basement, consult with an architect, builder, or licensed plumber about your plans. Be sure to obtain a full estimate for the work before proceeding.

If tying into existing lines below floor level is not practical or feasible, consider a sewage ejector. This is an electric pump attached to a holding tank. Sewage entering the tank from the bathroom is pumped up through a discharge pipe to a point where the pipe ties into the main house drain. The effective rise for the discharge pipe is about 10 feet—enough to reach the next level of your house. Sewage ejectors vary according to the size of the holding tank and the capacity of the pump motor. Expect to pay between $750 to $1,500 for an installed system.

You also must tie new drains to existing vent stacks, or install a new stack. Often, the easiest way is to run the new vent stack alongside the exterior of your house in an inconspicuous location.

➤ *In this 5x7 bathroom, mirrors stretching wall to wall and countertop to ceiling not only visually expand the space but also increase light by creating "double" the windows. The illusion is enhanced by walls completely covered by a striking design—in this case checkerboard-patterned wallpaper. A space-saving, 18-inch-wide sink leaves valuable counter space.*

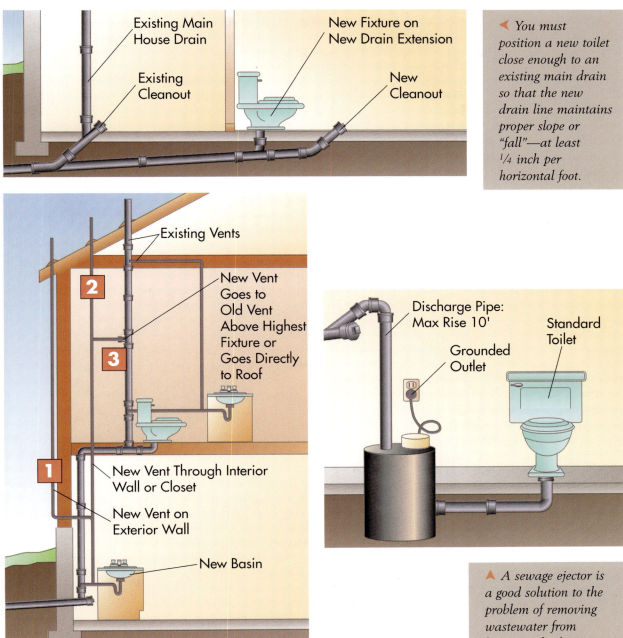

Existing Main House Drain

Existing Cleanout

New Fixture on New Drain Extension

New Cleanout

Existing Vents

2

New Vent Goes to Old Vent Above Highest Fixture or Goes Directly to Roof

3

1

New Vent Through Interior Wall or Closet

New Vent on Exterior Wall

New Basin

Discharge Pipe: Max Rise 10'

Grounded Outlet

Standard Toilet

◄ *You must position a new toilet close enough to an existing main drain so that the new drain line maintains proper slope or "fall"—at least $1/4$ inch per horizontal foot.*

▲ *There are three possibilities for locating a vent stack for newly installed basement plumbing fixtures. One method is to run the new stack along the home's exterior siding (1). Inside the house, the new vent stack can be hidden in an out-of-the-way location, such as an upstairs closet, and run out through the roof (2), or it can be connected to an existing vent stack (3).*

▲ *A sewage ejector is a good solution to the problem of removing wastewater from basement bathrooms. The ejector features a pump for elevating wastewater to a point where the pump's discharge pipe can connect to an existing main drain.*

Lighting

Planning a lighting scheme is especially important in a basement. Building codes typically require a living area to have windows with a total square footage of not less than 8 percent of the square footage of the floor area. In basements, this is not always possible, and codes allow exceptions for these rooms. The fact that window area is regulated by building codes, however, underscores the importance of light to a home's interior.

Basement rooms, especially in standard basements, rely on artificial lighting. There are four types of artificial light to consider when planning:

■ *Ambient, or general light* is soft, diffuse light provided by all lighting sources including daylight from windows. Create ambient light with indirect lighting fixtures, such as wall sconces that direct light upward where it bounces off the ceiling. Lamps with dark shades also direct light upward. Ambient light makes important contributions to a room's mood. If possible, place fixtures on rheostat switches (dimmers) to control the amount of ambient light.

■ *Downlighting* is cast by ceiling fixtures, such as pendant, recessed, and track lights, and by fluorescent light panels in suspended ceilings. Downlighting also creates ambient light. Codes usually dictate that at least one general lighting fixture be accessible by a light switch placed at the entry to a room. For basements, place a switch at the head and the bottom of the stairway for controlling lights within the stairwell. Allow one 60-watt fixture for every 10 feet of stair run. Locate switches for other room lights at the bottom of the stairs and at the entry to each individual room.

In basements with low ceiling height, pendant light fixtures that hang down from the ceiling may not be practical. Choose recessed or flush-mounted lights instead. To ensure adequate light, allow at least 1 watt per square foot of floor area with pendant and track lights and 1½ watts per square foot with recessed lights.

■ *Task lighting* is aimed at a specific area to help you perform such activities as reading, sewing, playing games, and working on hobbies. Task lighting is provided by movable desk and table lamps, under-counter light fixtures, and ceiling- or wall-mounted spotlights. Most tasks require 150 watts of incandescent or 40 watts of fluorescent light. For prolonged reading, allow 200 to 300 watts of incandescent or 60 to 80 watts of fluorescent light. For countertops and workbenches, provide 120 watts of incandescent or 20 watts of fluorescent lighting for each 3 running feet of work surface.

■ *Accent lighting* is similar to task lighting as it is aimed in a particular direction and is intended to illuminate a specific place or object. Unlike task lighting, which helps accomplish certain activities, accent lighting is used as a decorative element and is employed in sophisticated lighting schemes to highlight a work of art, emphasize a wall texture, or impart a sense of drama to a particular portion of a room.

▲ *Strategically placed recessed lighting helps illuminate specific work surfaces, such as counters and desktops. The three mini-spotlights above the counter in this basement wet bar can pivot slightly to focus light on different areas.*

> A comfortable family room becomes even more homey with a fake window. What appears to be a generous window is actually a frame covered with shutters. Behind the shutters is a fluorescent light fixture and a translucent diffusion screen that gives the illusion of daylight.

> A pair of floor lamps flanking a pull-out sofa-bed create good light for reading or doing crossword puzzles. They also bathe the room in soft, ambient light. Floor lamps provide flexibility and are easily moved if the scheme is rearranged.

Stairs

Gaining access to basement rooms is a major consideration. Stairs may need to be moved or reconfigured to make them safe or to allow basement rooms to be designed sensibly. The appearance of the stairway makes an important contribution to the overall interior design scheme of basement rooms.

Building codes have two sets of criteria for stairways. For primary stairways, such as those leading from the ground level to the upper level of a two-story house, there are rules governing the size of the treads, the risers, and the railings. For secondary stairways, such as those leading to an unfinished basement, the codes are less strict. When converting an unfinished basement to living area, you'll need to upgrade the stairway to meet the requirements of primary stairs.

Typical requirements for primary stairs include the following:
- 8 1/4-inch maximum height for risers
- 9-inch minimum depth for treads
- 32-inch minimum stair width between handrails
- 80-inch minimum headroom
- 34-inch minimum height for the handrail (measured above the tread at the riser)

Codes differ on the necessity and placement of balusters, but balusters greatly increase the safety of stairways, especially if you have small children in the household. Place balusters no more than 4 inches apart, measured horizontally and on-center. For added safety, consider enclosing the stairway with a solid wall that extends at least to the height of the handrail.

If your existing stairs are not suitable for a primary stairway, consider rebuilding them. To do so may require reconfiguring the stairway or moving the first-floor access door. Because the location of the stairs is important to the final layout of basement rooms, you should plan carefully. You may want to consult with an architect or other design professional to make sure the finished stairway

▲ *A typical secondary stairway (top) leading to an unfinished basement features steep steps and a minimal handrail. Reconfigured for a living area, this primary stairway (above) is less steep and makes a graceful entrance to basement rooms. The area underneath the stairway has been enclosed and turned into a closet.*

works well with the other ideas you have for your basement rooms.

For convenient storage, consider enclosing the triangular space beneath a stairway and adding a closet or a series of pull-out drawers.

> *This simple but well-planned stairway takes advantage of a corner to make an unobtrusive entry into the basement living area. The corner post is a structural element that makes an especially firm base for the handrail.*

◄ *A stairway needn't be dull. This lively version is inset with glass block that continues as a decorative band around the room. Using a solid wall makes the stairway especially safe for small children, and the glass block allows light to reach the stairs.*

Fireplaces

Fireplaces add great ambiance to any room. This is especially true in a basement, where a hearth can transform even the darkest, dreariest space into a warm and inviting living area. Fireplace units come in three basic types:

■ A "true" fireplace is designed to burn wood in a firebox made of heat-resistant masonry or metal. An all-masonry fireplace is made on-site by hand. While good-looking, it is very heavy and needs substantial support in the form of its own perimeter footing. This requirement makes all-masonry fireboxes impractical for retrofitting in existing basements. Proper planning, however, will ensure that the correct foundation support is provided in the basements of newly constructed homes. Often, a fireplace footing is made to support the weight of another fireplace at the next level of the home. The two flues are separate but run side-by-side in a single chimney.

Prefabricated units made of metal come ready for installation and are a cost-effective alternative to all-masonry fireplaces. They do not require additional floor support and are surrounded by conventional wood framing covered with drywall. Often, a veneer made of brick, stone, or other suitable material is added. Another type of metal firebox, called zero clearance, features double-walled, insulated construction that allows framing materials to be placed directly against the unit. Keep in mind that these units can be large and a bit unwieldy. Before ordering a prefabricated firebox, be sure you can get it into the basement.

Smoke in either type of fireplace exits through a flue pipe made of metal or fireproof clay tiles. Building codes require the flue of wood-burning fireplaces to exit nearly straight up through the roof. You'll need to make sure you have clearance from the basement to an exit point on the roof to install a proper flue—a process that means running the flue up through existing living areas. In this case, the flue is enclosed in a "chase"—framed walls covered with drywall. Careful planning is required to ensure the chase is not intrusive. An alternative is to run the flue on the exterior of the home—not the most attractive proposition.

◄ *Gas fireplaces are especially suited to remodeling projects. This unit includes power-assisted venting—a fan inside the vent helps exhaust combustion by-products. The fan permits the installation of small, 3-inch-diameter vent pipes in runs up to 50 feet in length.*

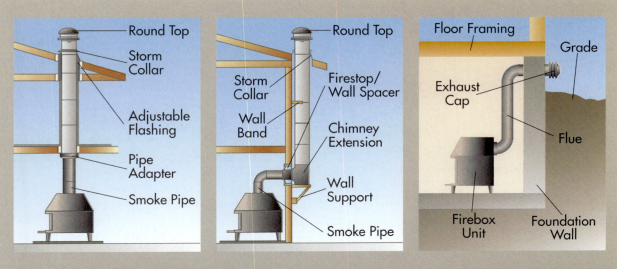

Venting a Wood-burning Heater

A wood-burning heater or fireplace vents directly up through the roof (left), *or along the outside of the house* (middle), *with a flue pipe that extends above the roofline. A gas-burning heater or fireplace* (right) *vents directly to the outside—a flue pipe that extends above the roofline is not necessary.*

■ Direct-vent gas fireplaces are increasingly popular because they are simple to install and produce no messy ash, making them ideal for retrofit situations. They burn either natural or LP gas and connect easily to a home's existing gas lines. A key advantage is that exhaust gases are vented to the outside through a relatively short length of flue pipe, and the pipe can make two right-angle turns without a loss of efficiency. In standard subterranean basements, vents exit through the above-grade portion of the foundation wall.

Direct-vent gas fireplaces come in many styles, sizes, and prices. Some units are designed to be enclosed by framed walls and finish materials. Others are completely freestanding and require no additional finish materials.

Gas fireplaces generate heat and, when activated, will keep basement rooms warm in colder months. One benefit of this type of fireplace is that it will produce heat in the event of an electrical failure. Although blowers and other accessories may not work, the gas burner units will function reliably during a power outage.

■ Ventless gas fireplaces burn so efficiently that they require no venting, making them ideal for retrofit situations. Until recently, however, many states banned ventless technology because the units created a health hazard. They tended to reduce the amount of available oxygen in the rooms they occupied. Today, most ventless gas fireplaces are required to include an oxygen depletion sensor (ODS), a safety feature that warns if oxygen levels in the room are becoming dangerously low.

Because these units are ventless, all heat produced is retained within the house. This makes the ventless gas fireplace highly energy-efficient. Like vented gas fireplaces, ventless units will continue to work in the event of a power failure.

When adding a fireplace to an existing basement room, the unit must sit out from the foundation walls and occupy floor space, an important consideration when planning basement room. Often, the area to either side of the fireplace unit is framed flush with the face of the fireplace and the space converted to shelves, cabinets, or other storage.

If you plan to include a fireplace, be sure to check local building codes. Most codes require a permit and periodic visits from the building inspector during the fireplace installation.

Planning Your New Space

Address all details to get a finished basement that's all you hoped for.

Wish lists are wonderful things. They allow flights of fancy to a place where everything is perfect. Turning these dreams into reality, however, requires a complete, workable plan. The plan for your basement conversion should list the intended uses of the space, a detailed list of items required, and a budget for materials and labor. Be sure to include any necessary repairs in your plan.

Include a scale drawing of the existing space with your plan. (Grid paper is included in the "Room Arranging Kit," on pages 94–95 of this book.) Drawn as seen from above, this is called a plan view; it should include details such as placement of stairs, windows, and heating/cooling equipment, and notations regarding problems—an existing window in a planned bedroom, for example, that doesn't meet egress requirements (page 50).

Occasionally, posts, ducts, pipes, and other obstacles complicate basement plans. Carefully map the location of obstructions on the plan view, and take them into account while planning. Moving a partition wall a couple of feet, for example, may allow you to incorporate a structural post within the wall, effectively camouflaging it. Locating a half-bath next to a furnace may allow you to build a single partition wall that encloses the bathroom and also creates a service closet that hides the mechanical equipment.

As a planning aide, you may also want to create scale views of the basement interior walls from the side to indicate these potential problems and to illustrate proposed solutions.

If your plans include alterations to the exterior, you may want to do exterior views, too. Doing a scale drawing that incorporates all the proposed changes will give you a good idea of what your house will look like when the project is complete.

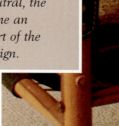

▶ *When it came time to remodel their basement, the owners of this suburban house chose to emphasize—rather than hide—the room's structural components. By painting metal support posts glossy black and keeping floor and wall finishes neutral, the posts became an integral part of the interior design.*

Special Considerations for Basements

One of the least glamorous tasks in planning a basement conversion is identifying and solving problems. Doing this, however, helps secure the success of your project. Check your plan against this list of special considerations for basements.

- Dealing with low ceilings (see "Ceilings," pages 46-49).
- Adding egress windows for bedrooms (see "Window and Doors," pages 50-53).
- Ensuring stairways conform to building codes (see "Stairs," pages 72-73).
- Solving moisture problems (see "Keeping Basements Dry," pages 54-63).
- Choosing suitable finishes for basement surfaces (see "Refining the Space," pages 36-45).
- Compensating for floors that slope toward a floor drain (see "Installing a Plywood Subfloor," page 40).
- Hiding or camouflaging furnaces, water heaters, and other mechanical equipment (see "Mapping the Changes," pages 82-89).
- Covering exposed overhead joists, pipes, ducts, and wires (see "Ceilings," pages 46–49).
- Adding sound insulation to block noise from rooms above (see "Sound Insulation," page 49).
- Creating adequate sources of ambient lighting and task lighting (see "Lighting," pages 70–71).
- Supplying a sufficient number of electrical outlets and telephone jacks.

You'd be wise to consider all the options before committing to a final design. You may decide to consult an architect or other design professional who can help you make informed choices and help find solutions to tricky problems.

> *Installing a sunken patio next to the foundation of a standard basement opens up the lower portion of your home with a modified walkout. Although expensive excavation is required, the cost often is compensated by the gain in light-filled living areas. Because a sunken patio is actually a pit rather than a true walk-out, it is essential to provide an adequate drainage system.*

Working with A **Design Professional**

The job of a professional designer is to create a space that meets your needs. A professional's expertise and experience allows him or her to offer fresh ideas, anticipate code restrictions, and deal with unusual problems. If the cost of hiring a pro seems prohibitive, consider that professionals can help save on overall costs by contributing to the efficiency of the project, organizing and managing work flow, and helping to avoid expensive mistakes. Many pros are willing to work as consultants for an hourly fee.

When working with a professional, good communication is key to achieving your goals. To help express your ideas, start a clipping folder. Use it to keep articles and photographs cut from magazines that show ideas and design details that appeal to you. Add product brochures or advertisements that you can share with your designer. A good designer is interested in your lifestyle and should ask questions about how you live, your daily routine, and your project goals.

Three types of design professionals are available for helping work on a basement project. Although they have specialized areas of expertise, most professionals are well-versed in all phases of design and can help create a comprehensive plan.

■ Architects work primarily with structure and reorganization of space. They are familiar with many types of building materials, finishes, and appliances, and have thorough knowledge of structural, electrical, plumbing, heating, ventilation, and air conditioning systems. Plans that include structural changes to your house and that need to be reviewed by your local building and planning commission should bear the stamp of a professional architect or structural engineer. Architects charge a percentage of the total cost of the project, usually 10 to 15 percent. If you hire them on an hourly basis, they charge $50 to $125 per hour. For a listing of architects in your area, look in the Yellow Pages of your phone directory, or try the internet search engine offered by the American Institute of Architects at http://www.e-architect.com/reference/home.asp.

■ Interior designers work with colors, wall finishes, fabrics, floor coverings, furnishings, lighting, and accessories to personalize a space and create a look that appeals to their clients. Increasingly, interior designers are familiar with building codes and structural requirements and can make recommendations for placement of partition walls, plumbing hookups, electrical outlets, and architectural details such as built-in storage units, moldings, door styles and sizes, and windows. If necessary, however, project plans must be approved by local building and planning commission. Structural changes require the stamp of a structural engineer or registered architect. Extensive remodeling projects may be subject to periodic inspection by the local building inspector. Interior designers certified by the American Society of Interior Designers (ASID) must demonstrate an ongoing knowledge of materials, building codes, government regulations, safety standards, and the latest products. For more information, visit the ASID web site at http://www.asid.org.

■ Design/build teams offer complete project management from initial design to completion of construction. Their involvement ensures that they are thoroughly familiar with the building methods and techniques specified by the project plan. Design/build teams may not offer the services of a registered architect. Therefore, structural modifications will require the approval of an architect or structural engineer. Design/build teams rarely offer interior design services.

Basic **Strategies**

Not all basement conversions involve large, start-to-finish remodeling projects. Some other strategies include the following:

■ Using minimal treatments. You can convert a basement to a basic living area with a minimum of effort and expense. If the room is dry and has adequate headroom, simply paint walls and add a few pieces of furniture to make the space livable. This simple strategy works well for creating a child's playroom, a simple game room with a pool table or ping pong table, or an exercise room. Use paints made specifically for concrete to cover walls and floors. To camouflage the overhead tangle of joists, pipes, and wires, paint the ceiling area a single color. A paint sprayer makes this job fast and efficient. Consider bright colors to help reflect light. Consider adding window treatments, folding screens to hide mechanical equipment, or some cushioned furniture to soften the hardness of concrete walls and floors.

■ Altering space. When your plans include a specific use that requires creating a distinct room, such as a bedroom or bathroom, you'll need to construct partition walls. These walls can be placed

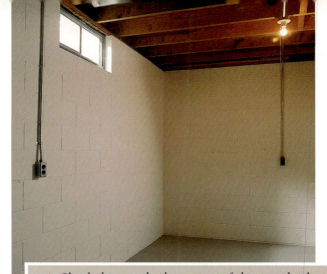

▲ *Slowly but surely the owners of this standard basement will convert the space to living quarters, doing a portion of the work each year.*

almost anywhere, and can include doors. To reduce sound transmission, insulate stud walls and spaces between overhead joists with fiberglass batting.

Using a partition wall also allows you to finish just a portion of the basement. Create an office just off the stairs, for example, and leave the rest of the basement unfinished.

■ Doing the work in stages. By doing just a portion of the work each year, you'll keep annual out-of-pocket expenses lower, allowing you to complete the project as family finances permit. You should still begin with a complete plan, especially with newly constructed homes. If you decide to build a guest suite in the basement, for example, but won't complete the work for several years, have all plumbing and electrical hookups roughed-in before the basement slab is poured. Extending your home's systems later may mean tearing out concrete and other expensive alterations that could have been avoided.

◀ *This basement needed only durable carpeting and painted walls to become a child's haven. Tack boards are an imaginative and useful wall treatment.*

▶ *The owners of this 19th-centu... did little to their basement except... the stone foundation walls and a... furniture. The result is a charmin... summer dining room.*

Mapping The Changes

Perfect the design for your new basement rooms using a three stage process: First, draw up a plan of the existing space, then sketch in all the anticipated modifications, and, finally, add furnishings. Even if you're planning to hire an architect or interior designer, sketch your preliminary ideas. Your sketches will service as the basis for additional planning.

The map of your existing basement should be drawn to scale with all details noted (see page 76 for tips on doing a plan view).

Make several photocopies so you can test a variety of design options and solutions to problems on paper.

Once you decide on a general layout for the space, use the "Room Arranging Kit" (see pages 90-95) to add room furnishings. If you can't get the pieces to fit, try going back to step two and making additional modifications to room sizes and configurations.

To give you an idea of how the process works, this section follows the planning process for several basements conversions.

Family Space

By installing a partition wall along the length of this basement, the space is divided into two areas—a living area and an unfinished space to house the water heater, furnace, and laundry area. The partition wall is placed directly beneath a structural steel beam so that the beam and supporting columns are hidden inside the new wall. Additional partition walls enclose a new half bath and storage area.

The half bath is located close to the washer and dryer so the bath fixtures will connect to the existing drain and vent system. In this case, the concrete floor must be broken, trenched, and a new drain line installed to reach the existing sewer line. Once connected, the trench can be repaired with concrete patching material.

In the living area, concrete basement walls are furred out with 1x2s, insulated with rigid insulation board, and covered with drywall (see "Walls," pages 42–45). The stairs are widened to make the stairway more architecturally pleasing. Built-ins, base cabinets in the main room, and shelves in the storage room maximize storage space.

Furnishings are simple and comfortable. A sofa, two chairs, and two small tables create a small grouping in front of the television.

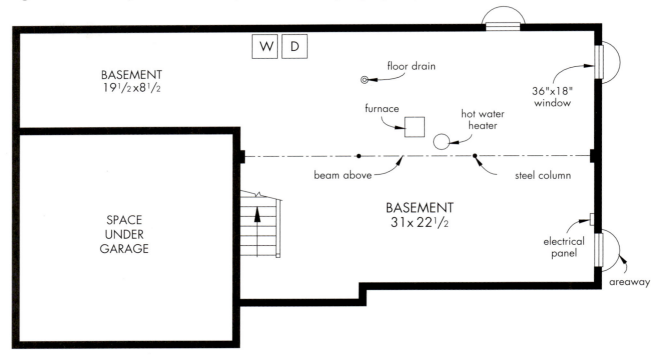

BASEMENT
19½x8½

W D

floor drain

furnace

hot water heater

36"x18" window

beam above

steel column

SPACE UNDER GARAGE

BASEMENT
31x 22½

electrical panel

areaway

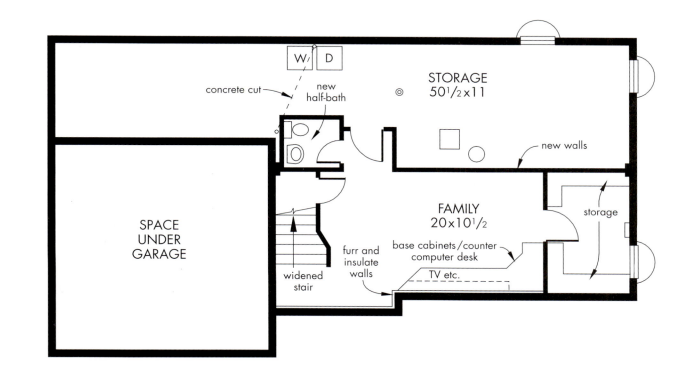

W/ D

concrete cut

new
half-bath

STORAGE
50 1/2 x 11

new walls

SPACE
UNDER
GARAGE

FAMILY
20 x 10 1/2

storage

furr and
insulate
walls

base cabinets/counter
computer desk

widened
stair

TV etc.

▲ *The finished family room features built-in cabinets for holding television and stereo equipment and a built-in desk for the computer workstation. The comfortable furniture grouping is perfect for watching TV, reading, or just relaxing.*

Shop and Laundry

This large unfinished basement features a centrally located stairway. By letting the steel beams and supporting columns help define the locations of parti-tion walls, the space is made into a series of smaller rooms, with the stairway descending into the central hobby room. The main goal—creating a workshop—is achieved by installing a partition wall that spans the width of the basement. This wall features a double door for moving large pieces of material, machinery, or finished projects in and out of the shop. In addition, an exterior access door is added at the end of the shop. This type of door requires a

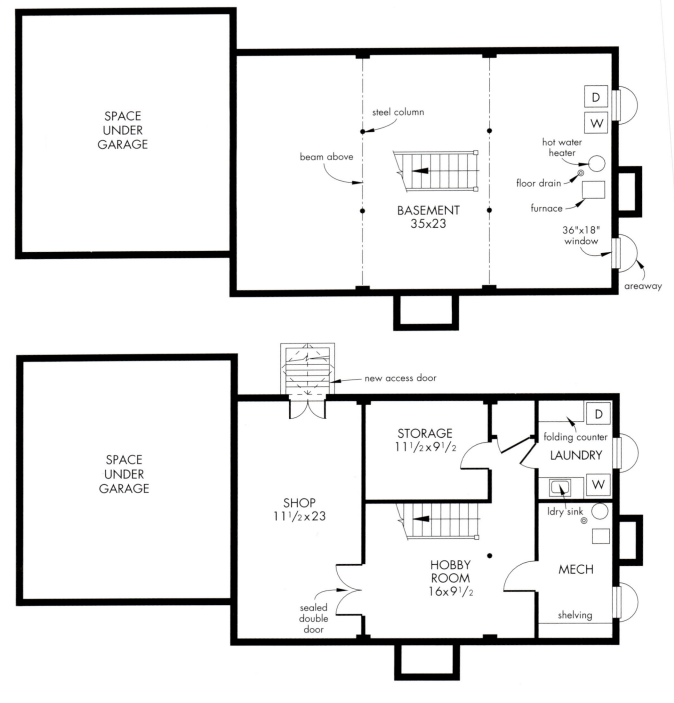

SPACE UNDER GARAGE

steel column

beam above

BASEMENT 35x23

D

W

hot water heater

floor drain

furnace

36"x18" window

areaway

SPACE UNDER GARAGE

new access door

SHOP 11½x23

STORAGE 11½x9½

folding counter

LAUNDRY

D

W

ldry sink

MECH

HOBBY ROOM 16x9½

shelving

sealed double door

small excavation to accommodate stairs leading down to the basement, and a passageway cut into the existing foundation. Before attempting this modification, have a qualified architect or structural engineer verify that the location of the passageway will not jeopardize the integrity of the foundation or its ability to support the weight of the house. Side walls lining the excavation are made of poured concrete. The stairway is covered by lockable, insulated, steel bulkhead doors (see "Bulkhead Access Doors," page 52).

Other partition walls form a storage area, a generous laundry room with a wash tub and folding center, and an enclosure that hides the furnace and water heater from the hobby room. One side of the main stairway is closed with a partition wall, but the other side is left open to the hobby room. Although well-designed, this plan doesn't conceal all supporting posts, a single post remains exposed in the hobby room, a common compromise for basement spaces.

With the exception of the shop, the space is simply and inexpensively furnished. A work table, shelves, and a built-in desk keep the hobby room versatile and flexible. To minimize expense, the floor will be painted with heavy-duty floor enamel.

▲ *A bulkhead access door allows easy entry to the generous shop space. The area surrounding the existing interior stairway is outfitted with a work surface and storage cabinets that create space for a hobby area or a small home office.*

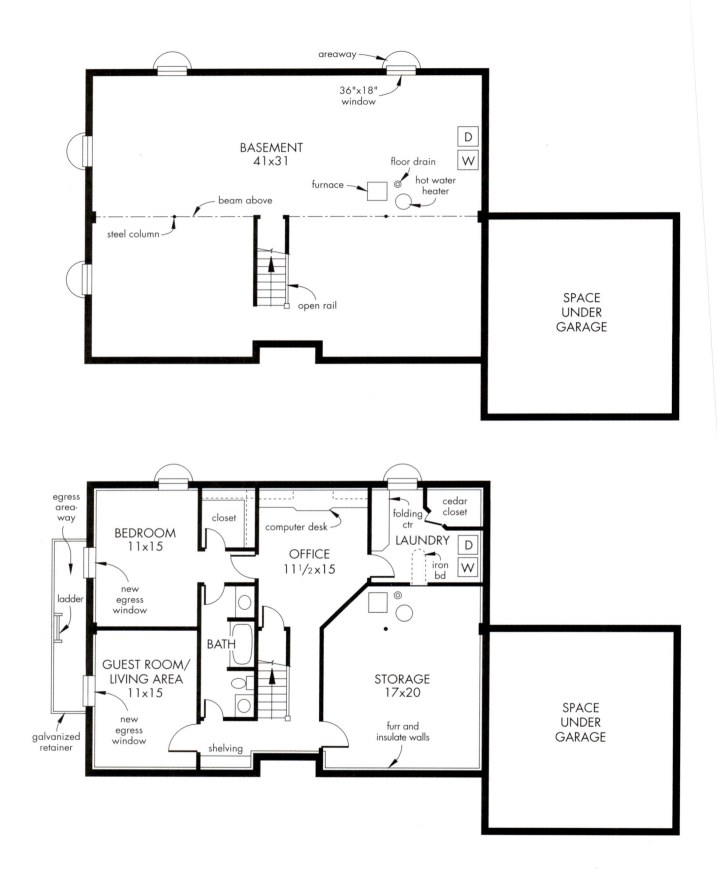

Basement floor plan (top):
BASEMENT 41x31
areaway
36"x18" window
D
W
floor drain
hot water heater
furnace
beam above
steel column
open rail
SPACE UNDER GARAGE

Lower floor plan (bottom):
egress area-way
BEDROOM 11x15
closet
computer desk
folding ctr
cedar closet
LAUNDRY
D
W
iron bd
OFFICE 11½x15
ladder
new egress window
BATH
GUEST ROOM/ LIVING AREA 11x15
new egress window
galvanized retainer
shelving
STORAGE 17x20
furr and insulate walls
SPACE UNDER GARAGE

Office and Bedroom

An open, unused standard basement is transformed into an all-purpose living area that includes a bedroom, a full bath, an office, a computer workstation, and a laundry room. There's even space for a generous storage area.

Because these rooms will be used on an everyday basis, all foundation walls are insulated and covered with drywall to present a smooth, even finish. The living area could be converted to a bedroom because the large excavated area permits the installation of egress windows for both rooms. Another benefit is the generous supply of daylight available to both rooms. One escape ladder built into the side of the excavation is all that's needed to meet safety requirements.

The bedroom is furnished with a queen-sized bed. The second room, if not used as a living area, has ample room for a sofa bed, giving the room flexibility to be used a second basement bedroom for additional guests.

▲ *Careful planning is required to ensure all plumbing drain lines can be connected to the existing main drain, and installing new drains requires cutting into the existing slab. Enlist the advice of a reliable plumbing professional to make sure it's done right.*

In-Law **Suite**

The unfinished walkout basement of this newly built house is big—nearly 2,000 square feet—and makes an ideal location for an in-law suite. Planning this space prior to construction of the house ensures that plumbing and electrical systems needed by the suite are already installed. This way, the work can be completed in stages, spreading the costs over several years until the project is complete. All windows and doors are installed during initial construction, with the exception of an additional window installed in the game room.

The plan incorporates almost all structural posts and support beams into partition walls. A bay window enclosure makes the bedroom especially appealing, and the large central window of the bay is sized for egress to comply with building codes. The suite includes a kitchenette that opens to a dining area. Stylish French doors lead to an outside patio. To make sure the patio receives enough daylight, a large deck that originally covered the French door entryway is scheduled to be shortened.

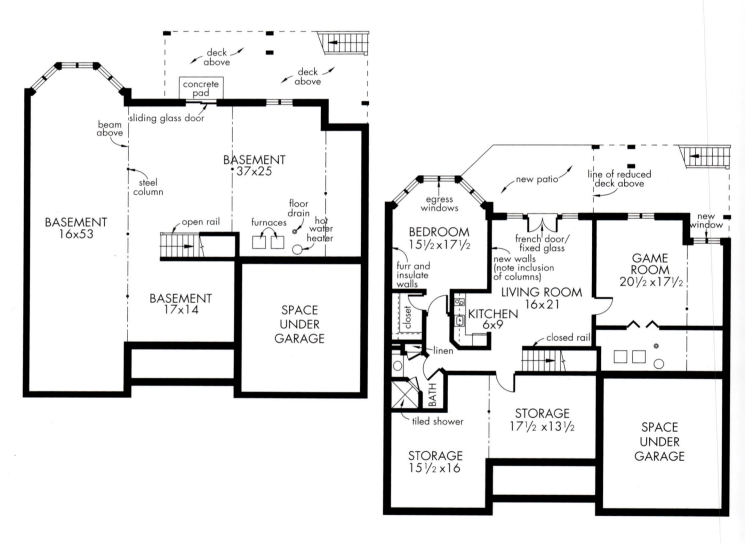

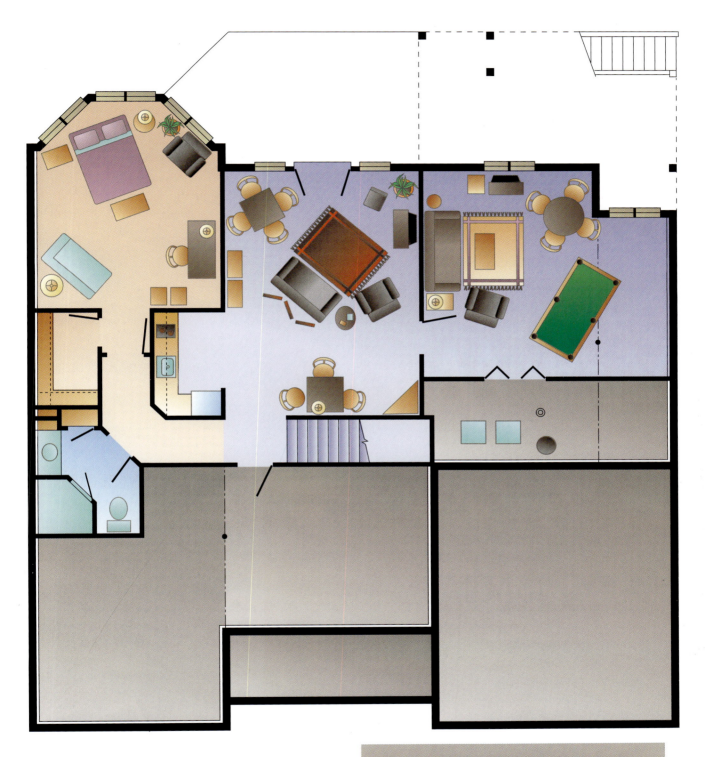

▲ A space this large can accommodate many pieces of furniture. There's room for a sofa and chair near the television, and a dining table with a corner hutch against the stairway. The hobby room holds a pool table and game table and four chairs, and the bedroom is amply furnished.

Room Arranging Kit

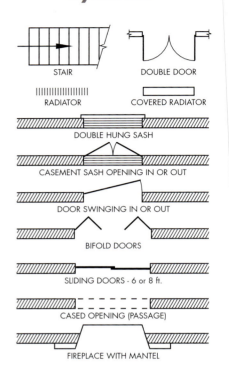

STAIR

DOUBLE DOOR

RADIATOR

COVERED RADIATOR

DOUBLE HUNG SASH

CASEMENT SASH OPENING IN OR OUT

DOOR SWINGING IN OR OUT

BIFOLD DOORS

SLIDING DOORS - 6 or 8 ft.

CASED OPENING (PASSAGE)

FIREPLACE WITH MANTEL

The key to creating an inviting, usable space is good placement of furnishings. Think about how you plan to use the space and choose the pieces—both furniture you have and items you'll add—needed to make the space work. Using the "Room Arranging Kit" on the following pages, work through these steps:

■ *Measure the room.* Plot it on the grid (pages 94-95) or on same-size grid paper. One square equals one foot of floor space. Use the architectural symbols (right) to mark doorways, stairs, and the like. Be sure to include all the features of space. Using dotted lines, mark key obstructions—such as low ductwork or lights.

■ *Use the furniture templates.* Trace or photocopy the appropriate items from the templates on the following pages, and cut them out with a crafts knife. If you have furniture or special items that need templates, measure them and draw them to the same scale—one square equals one foot—on grid paper.

■ *Find a focal point.* Physically, this is the cornerstone around which you build a furniture grouping; visually, it's the dramatic element that draw you into a room. If your room doesn't have a natural focus—such as a fireplace or built-in bookcases—substitute a large-scaled or boldly colored accessory, or freestanding wall units.

Here are a few tips to help you place furnishings:

■ *Direct traffic.* If traffic passes through a room, it doesn't have to run through the center. Think of your furnishings as walls or guideposts that can funnel traffic.

■ *Float furnishings.* Pull pieces away from walls into close-knit groupings with major seating no more than 8 feet apart.

■ *Keep convenience within reach.* Set a handy resting place—an end table, stack of books, or short cabinet—for drinks or books close to every seat.

■ *Maximize a small room.* Include a large-scale piece, such as an armoire or hefty love seat, for a feeling of grandeur. Use vertical storage in tight spaces.

■ *Fix low ceilings.* "Raise" a low ceiling with floor-to-ceiling window treatments and tall furniture. And allow for ceiling obstructions. Direct traffic away from or around these low-hanging items. (See right for height requirements.)

Finish Ceiling

Obstructions

Hallway and Bathrooms Min 7'

Pipes, Ducts, And Other Obstructions Min 6'8"

Habi Roon Min

Upholstered Furniture and Bedding

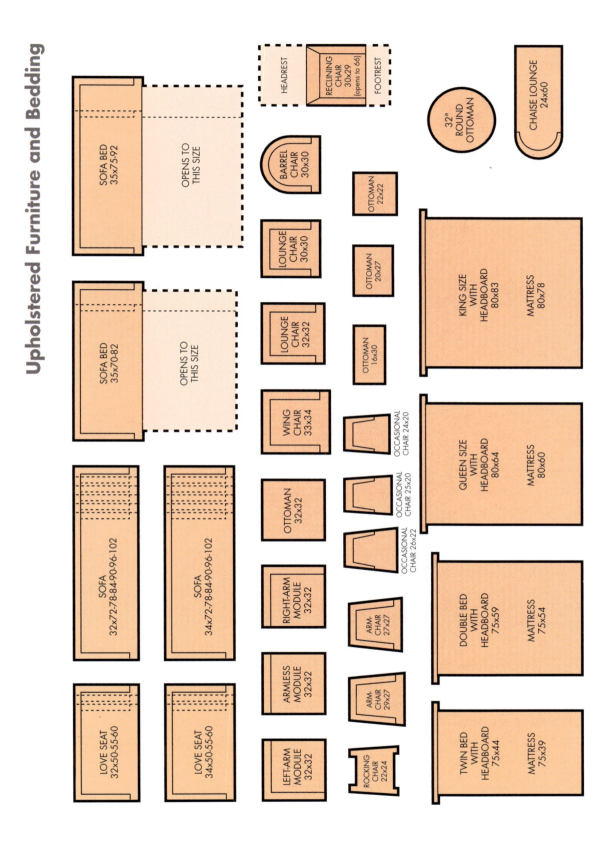

SOFA BED
35x75-92

OPENS TO
THIS SIZE

SOFA BED
35x70-82

OPENS TO
THIS SIZE

HEADREST

RECLINING
CHAIR
30x29
(opens to 66)

FOOTREST

BARREL
CHAIR
30x30

LOUNGE
CHAIR
30x30

LOUNGE
CHAIR
32x32

WING
CHAIR
33x34

OTTOMAN
32x32

RIGHT-ARM
MODULE
32x32

ARMLESS
MODULE
32x32

LEFT-ARM
MODULE
32x32

SOFA
32x72-78-84-90-96-102

SOFA
34x72-78-84-90-96-102

LOVE SEAT
32x50-55-60

LOVE SEAT
34x50-55-60

OTTOMAN
22x22

OTTOMAN
20x27

OTTOMAN
16x30

OCCASIONAL
CHAIR 24x20

OCCASIONAL
CHAIR 25x20

OCCASIONAL
CHAIR 26x22

ARM-
CHAIR
27x27

ARM-
CHAIR
29x27

ROCKING
CHAIR
22x24

32"
ROUND
OTTOMAN

CHAISE LOUNGE
24x60

KING SIZE
WITH
HEADBOARD
80x83

MATTRESS
80x78

QUEEN SIZE
WITH
HEADBOARD
80x64

MATTRESS
80x60

DOUBLE BED
WITH
HEADBOARD
75x59

MATTRESS
75x54

TWIN BED
WITH
HEADBOARD
75x44

MATTRESS
75x39

91

Room Arranging Kit

Use a photocopier to reproduce these cutout images at 100 percent of their original design. Work with the grid on pages 94-95.

Bathroom Fixtures and Exercise Equipment

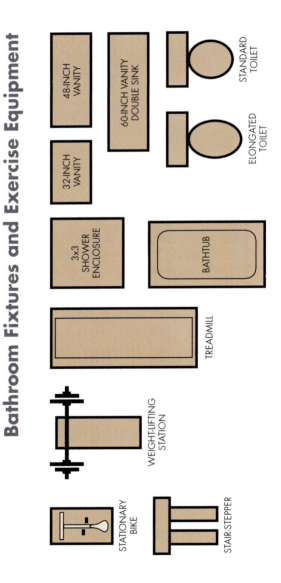

48-INCH VANITY

32-INCH VANITY

60-INCH VANITY DOUBLE SINK

STANDARD TOILET

ELONGATED TOILET

3x3 SHOWER ENCLOSURE

BATHTUB

TREADMILL

WEIGHT-LIFTING STATION

STATIONARY BIKE

STAIR-STEPPER

Occasional Tables and Special Pieces

COCKTAIL TABLE 28x66

DESK 30x60

DESK 25x50

COCKTAIL TABLE 22x60

BUFFET 21x60

STEREO CONSOLE 17x54

DESK 18x40

COCKTAIL TABLE 22x44

BREAKFRONT SECRETARY 19x72

COLOR TV 20x50

TABLE 22x28

COLOR TV 19x36

TABLE AND FLOOR LAMPS

TABLE 20x24

CONSOLE 20x40

DRESSING TABLE 22x44

TABLE 18x24

ROUND TABLE 40"

STOOL 18"

TABLE 16x22

BENCH 12x28

COLOR TV 20x42

SQUARE TABLE 20x20

ROUND TABLE 36"

CORNER CABINET 28x28

SQUARE TABLE 36x36

ROUND TABLE 24"

Dining Room Tables and Chairs

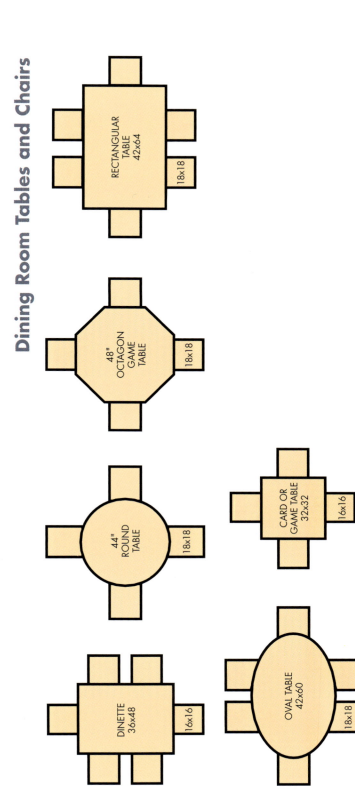

RECTANGULAR TABLE 42x64 — 18x18

48" OCTAGON GAME TABLE — 18x18

44" ROUND TABLE — 18x18

CARD OR GAME TABLE 32x32 — 16x16

DINETTE 36x48 — 16x16

OVAL TABLE 42x60 — 18x18

Interchangeable Storage Pieces and Special Pieces

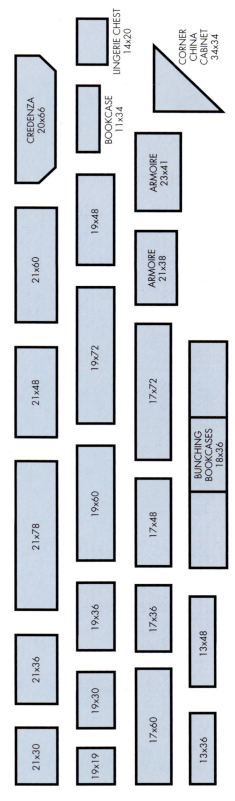

LINGERIE CHEST 14x20

CORNER CHINA CABINET 34x34

CREDENZA 20x66

BOOKCASE 11x34

ARMOIRE 23x41

ARMOIRE 21x38

19x48

21x60

21x48

19x72

17x72

21x78

19x60

17x48

BUNCHING BOOKCASES 18x36

19x36

17x36

21x36

19x30

13x48

21x30

19x19

17x60

13x36

Room Arranging Kit

Use a photocopier to reproduce this grid at its original size. Use the cutouts on pages 91–93 to help design your basement space. The scale of the grid is 1" equals 1'.

What Will It Cost?

Estimating costs and establishing a budget are essential to good planning.

A basement project can be as simple as finishing walls and floors, or as complex as creating a guest suite complete with bedroom, closets, bathroom, and sitting area. Deciding what to do often is directed by the cost of doing the project.

Another thing to consider is resale value. Upgrading your home by converting your basement to a living area will increase the value of your property and make your home more attractive to prospective buyers if you decide to sell. Each project increases home value at a different rate. For example, adding a bathroom is one of the most valuable improvements you can make. According to annual surveys of building contractors and real estate agents, a new bathroom can recoup more than 90 percent of the costs of construction. The home office is another high-value project, recovering more than 70 percent of construction costs. Keep in mind that you shouldn't overimprove your house by making it considerably more valuable than other houses in your neighborhood. Your proposed project should not increase the price of your home more than 15 percent of the average price of houses in your area. Then the cost of the upgrade will be easier to recover when you sell your home.

You probably won't undertake a basement project based on resale value alone. If you plan to live in your home for years to come, you decisions will be based more on increased livability and convenience than on resale value. Insist on quality materials and workmanship that will make your project a sound investment and an enjoyable space for years to come.

In this section are brief descriptions of popular basement remodeling projects, including pricing data from cost-estimate specialist, R.S. Means Company, Inc., Kingston, MA, a CMD Group Company. Their annual cost books and quarterly updates covering dozens of construction specialties, have been the most quoted standard for planning and estimating by the construction industry for over 57 years. For more information, contact R.S. Means at 1-800/334-3509.

How To Use This Chapter

Your project may include more than one of the projects outlined in this chapter. To estimate a final price, combine all the relevant costs. For example, the "Standard Half Bath" project described on page 100 lists all the materials and fixtures you'll need for a bathroom interior, but the number and size of partition walls will vary with your plans. For those costs, consult the "Partition Wall" project on page 107. Add everything together to get a final estimate.

Once you've arrived at some estimates, check the "Adjusting Costs" table on pages 108—109 The table allows you to adjust the estimates to your location.

Quick-Reference Table of Contents

Standard Basement

This project includes finishing a 20x24-foot portion of a larger basement. Improvements include adding basic wall surfaces, flooring, and a suspended ceiling. The project assumes that a stairway exists but that the area beneath the stairs will be enclosed and converted to a closet and the stairway outfitted with a railing and balusters.

The bare concrete walls are first prepared with 1x3 furring strips set on 16-inch centers. The space between the strips is insulated with rigid styrofoam insulation that matches the thickness of the furring. An electrical circuit is extended through the walls and includes six receptacles and terminal connections for two electrical baseboard heaters. The walls are then covered with ½-inch drywall that is taped, sanded, and painted.

The suspended ceiling system is composed of metal channels and prefinished 2x4-foot acoustical tile panels hung from the exposed floor joists above. The ceiling includes two light fixtures and the final price of this basement project includes installing the necessary wiring and switches. The flooring is 12x12-inch self-adhesive vinyl tiles.

After all surfaces are in place, the room is trimmed with pine casings and baseboards. The under-the-stairs closet includes a door and lock.

Cost for materials = $3,312

Total contractor's fee including materials = $9,026

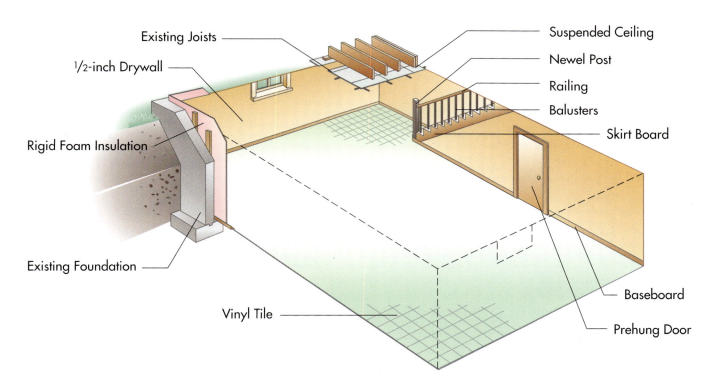

Existing Joists

½-inch Drywall

Rigid Foam Insulation

Existing Foundation

Vinyl Tile

Suspended Ceiling

Newel Post

Railing

Balusters

Skirt Board

Baseboard

Prehung Door

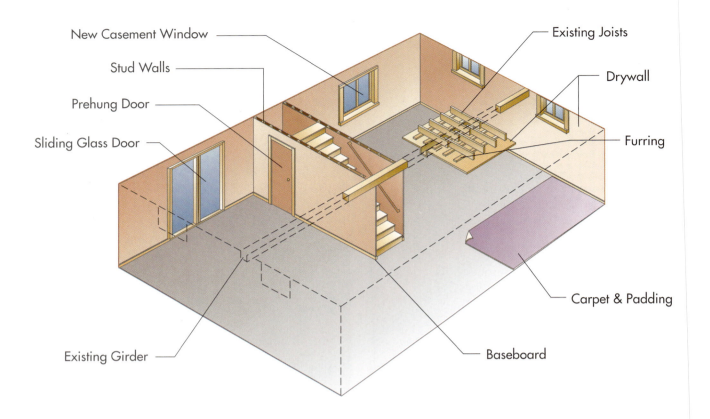

New Casement Window

Stud Walls

Prehung Door

Sliding Glass Door

Existing Joists

Drywall

Furring

Carpet & Padding

Existing Girder

Baseboard

Walkout Basement

Walkout basements make ideal living spaces. The walkout side of the space can be fitted with generous windows and glass doors to provide plenty of daylight. A walkout makes a good location for a spare bedroom—the space easily can be fitted with the egress window required by building codes.

The 24x40-foot walkout basement project illustrated here includes installing a large casement window and sliding glass door, partition walls that separate the space into two areas, a closet under the stairs, and a drywall ceiling.

The bare concrete walls are prepared with 1x3 furring strips set on 16-inch centers, then insulated with rigid styrofoam of the same thickness as the furring. An electrical circuit is extended through the walls and includes ten receptacles and terminal connections for four electrical baseboard heaters. The walls are then covered with ½-inch drywall.

For a completely finished appearance, the ceiling is covered with ½-inch drywall. Furring strips are first attached to the joists and shimmed where necessary to account for any sagging or bowing of the joists. If sagging is severe enough to require correction with "sister" joists, the costs will be higher. The drywall is attached, then all drywall surfaces are taped, sanded, and painted. For simplicity, it is assumed that all electrical wiring, plumbing, and ducts run above the bottom of the joists. If these systems need to be moved to make way for the drywall, figure some additional costs. The ceiling includes two light fixtures, and the final price of this project includes installing the necessary wiring and switches. The flooring is foam-backed carpet.

After all surfaces are in place, the room is trimmed with pine casings and baseboards. The under-the-stairs closet includes a door and lock.

Cost for materials = $6,715
Total contractor's fee including materials = $17,370

Fireplace

This project includes the installation of a prefabricated, freestanding, vented gas fireplace unit approximately 42 inches wide, 36 inches tall, and 22 inches deep. The unit uses either LP or natural gas that is supplied by the addition of a 15-foot run of ¾-inch pipe tied into an existing gas line. Because the unit sits out from an existing foundation wall, it must be enclosed in a 2x4 framework that is constructed before the fireplace is installed. The total depth of the framework takes into account the fireplace plus enough space to allow insulated, 5-inch diameter pipe from the rear-vented unit to exit the fireplace, turn 90 degrees, rise vertically for a distance of about 5 feet, and take another 90-degree turn to exit the foundation wall above grade. On the outside of the house, the vent pipe is finished with a heavy-duty aluminum baffled vent cap.

The total required depth for the framework is approximately 46 inches. Consider whether the amount of space required by the fireplace is in keeping with your plans for your basement room. Often, the space on either side of such an installation is enclosed with framing and turned into book shelves or storage cabinets. Creating shelves and cabinets is not included in the project price presented here.

Once built, the wood framework is covered with ½-inch drywall. The front of the enclosure is then covered with a brick veneer to a distance of about 4½ feet from the basement floor. The top of the veneer is finished with a 6-foot-long, laminated board featuring an oak veneer.

Cost for materials = $1,235
Total contractor's fee including materials = $3,140

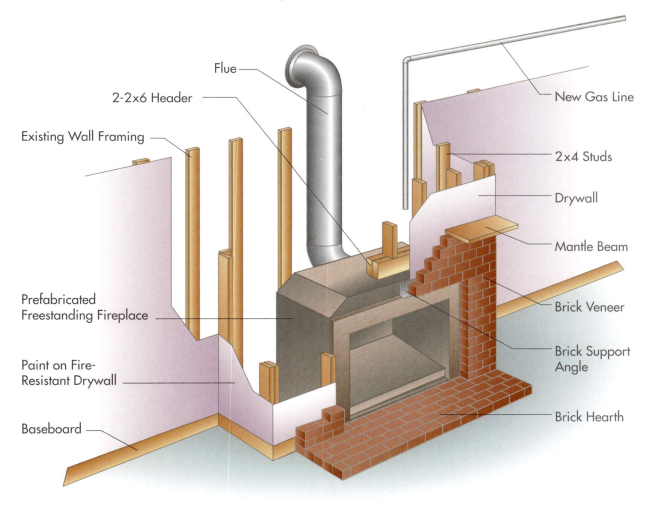

Flue

2-2x6 Header

Existing Wall Framing

New Gas Line

2x4 Studs

Drywall

Mantle Beam

Prefabricated Freestanding Fireplace

Brick Veneer

Brick Support Angle

Paint on Fire-Resistant Drywall

Brick Hearth

Baseboard

Standard Half Bath

Most of the components included in this 4x6-foot bath project are basic, modestly priced items that are readily available at home improvement centers. However, that doesn't mean your finished bathroom must be dull. Two of the materials—the vinyl flooring and the plastic laminate vanity countertop—come in a wide array of colors and styles. Paint the walls an interesting color and your bathroom addition will be a champion of fine style.

The basic plumbing fixtures for a standard half bath are a vanity sink and a toilet. There are a number of sink sizes available, but an 18-inch, round, cast-iron unit coated with porcelain is a fine, functional sink that will last for years. A two-piece vitreous china toilet is a standard item at any home improvement or plumbing supply store. Add 25 percent to the cost of the toilet if you prefer a color other than white. This project calls for matching chrome-plated fittings, faucet, and shut-off valves under the vanity sink. The project price includes the cost of cutting the concrete slab floor and installing a 10-foot-long run of new drain line that connects to the existing main drain line. After the new line is installed, the slab is repaired.

The flooring specified is economical and durable vinyl sheet flooring. Vinyl sheet flooring glues down easily over clean, dry concrete, but the surface of the concrete must be completely free of cracking or chipping. Imperfections should be removed with grinding equipment and cracks and recesses filled with hydraulic cement or leveling compound and trowled completely smooth. To ensure proper installation, it is recommended that a plywood subfloor be installed on 2x4 sleepers. The project price includes either finishing the concrete slab or installing a plywood subfloor.

The vanity cabinet is a standard 30-inch model with a laminate plastic top. Included in the cost of the project is the installation of a new medicine cabinet and chrome-plated towel bars.

Basement Bathrooms

Any bathroom project requires careful planning. This is especially true in a basement, where access to the necessary drains and vent stacks may restrict the bathroom to a few locations. If your basement is affected by high humidity and condensation, you may want to consider a ventilation system for drawing moisture from the bathroom and directing it outside the house. Always check with your building department for information on permits, codes, and other regulations before installing a new bathroom. For more information, see pages 68–69.

Cost for materials = $1,135

Total contractor's fee including materials = $2,669

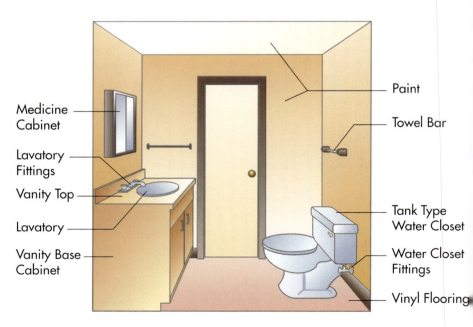

Medicine Cabinet
Lavatory Fittings
Vanity Top
Lavatory
Vanity Base Cabinet
Paint
Towel Bar
Tank Type Water Closet
Water Closet Fittings
Vinyl Flooring

Ceramic Tile Tub Surround

Drywall

Sliding Shower Door

Ceramic Tile Wainscoting

Bathtub

Tank Type Water Closet

Paint

Drywall

Plate Glass Mirror

Lavatory Fittings

Lavatory

Vanity Top

Vanity Base Cabinet

Ceramic Tile

Standard Full Bath

This 7x8-foot bathroom project features top-quality fixtures, ceramic tile on the walls and floor, and custom accessories. The fixtures include an 18-inch vanity sink made of porcelain enameled cast-iron, a one-piece floor-mounted toilet, and a porcelain enameled cast-iron bathtub. The faucets, spout, diverter, and shower head are all top-quality items. Included in the list of installed items is a sliding shower door with tempered safety glass.

Setting the style in this bathroom is 1-inch ceramic tile on the floors and 4-inch ceramic tiles set wainscot-high on the walls. Carefully installed, ceramic tile is one of the most beautiful and durable building materials. Tiles come in many colors and styles, and you should visit a tile supply store to study the varieties. Some tiles are not readily available and may take several weeks for delivery. Consult with your contractor about buying tiles, ordering the right shapes and qualities, and having them delivered on schedule. If you decide to pur- chase the tiles yourself, make sure they are removed from the list of items provided by your contractor.

This project includes a vanity fitted with a marble countertop, a medicine cabinet with a built-in light fixture, stainless steel towel bars, electrical lighting fixtures and switches, and a ground-fault circuit interrupter (GFCI) electrical outlet.

The project price includes the cost of cutting the slab floor and installing a 10-foot-long run of new drain line that connects to the existing main drain line. After the new line is installed, the concrete slab is repaired.

Cost for materials = $3,785

Total contractor's fee including materials = $7,835

See Also:

See also: "Partition Wall," page 107

Sauna Room

Adding a sauna is a popular home improvement. Although it can be classified as a luxury item, many people believe saunas offer health benefits, such as reducing stress.

Most saunas come prepackaged with all necessary equipment, controls, and interior finish materials. You need to provide structural walls—a framed shell—and hookups for electricity. Although a sauna is not big, it can be an awkward fit within the existing scheme of your house. A basement offers a good solution. If you take advantage of a corner location, then two of the shell walls are already in place, ready to covered with finish materials. The overhead floor joists allow attachment of ceiling materials. Saunas don't require daylight, so locating one near a window isn't necessary. Unlike a steam bath, saunas use dry heat, so plumbing and a floor drain aren't required.

Prefinished saunas come in many different styles and prices. Inexpensive units uses walls made of hemlock, spruce, or fir. More expensive ones have walls of cedar or redwood. Sauna accessories, such as back rests, interior light fixtures, towel bars, and timer controls, are additional costs and are not included in this project.

This example calls for a moderately priced, 6x6-foot unit with two benches and a safety railing. Because this project cannot anticipate your exact location, the final price includes construction of four shell walls and installation of ceiling joists. If your sauna location permits the use of existing basement walls or ceiling joists, you can reduce costs by 10 percent.

For energy efficiency, the shell walls are made of 2x4s with fiberglass insulation. The shell walls should be constructed carefully so they are level, plumb, and square—building the walls on a sloped concrete slab floor without shimming could cause misalignment of prefabricated components. The door is made with insulated and tempered safety glass. The floor finish is of 2x2-inch ceramic tiles grouted directly onto the concrete slab. This size tile is considered slip-proof.

A heater for a sauna runs on normal 110-volt household current. There is no need to install a separate circuit. A certified electrician should make all service connections without complications.

Cost for materials = $4,945

Total contractor's fee including materials = $8,187

Prefabricated Sauna w/Heater & Control

Safety Railing

Door w/Tempered Insulated Glass Window

Ceiling: 2x6 Joists
6" Insulation
1/2" Fire-Resistant Drywall

Floor: 2'x2' Ceramic Tile

Wall Framing:
2x4 Studs & Plates
2-2x6 Headers
3 1/2" Insulation
1/2" Fire-Resistant Drywall Each Side

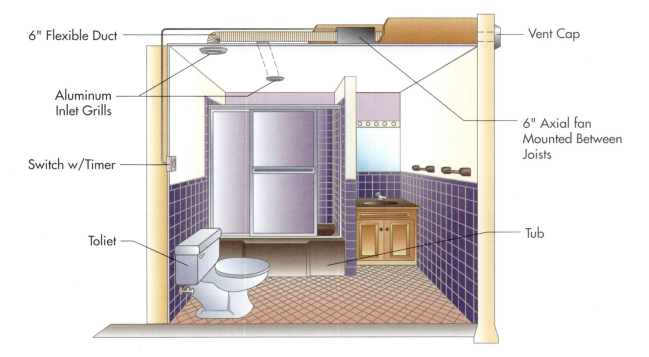

Labels on the diagram:
- 6" Flexible Duct
- Aluminum Inlet Grills
- Switch w/Timer
- Toliet
- Vent Cap
- 6" Axial fan Mounted Between Joists
- Tub

Ventilation
System

Bathrooms produce lots of humidity. If you are planning to add a bathroom to your basement, you should consider installing a ventilation system that removes humid air to the outside of your house. To do so, you'll need to be able to run ductwork from the bathroom to the side of your house. If your new bathroom is located next to an exterior wall, access is easy. If not, you'll need the advice of a contractor or heating and cooling professional to determine if it is feasible to run the ductwork through joists to an outside wall.

Ventilation fans are manufactured in many types and configurations. Some include lighting fixtures or infrared heaters. They are wall or ceiling mounted, and the motors are axial (propeller-type) or centrifugal (squirrel-cage type). In all cases they must be true vented fans, exhausting air to the outside of the house. Some exhaust fans merely exhaust air into the space between ceiling joists. These should not be used for a basement bathroom.

Fans are rated by the amount of air they are able to move, a figure given as cubic feet per minute (cfm). According to the Home Ventilating Institute, an exhaust fan should be able to exchange bathroom air at least eight times per hour. Systems with long runs of ductwork and that have several turns or elbows create more air-flow resistance and require larger capacity fans. Consult a contractor or heating and cooling professional for a recommendation.

Fans also have noise ratings, and can range from one sone (the quietest) to more than four sones. Fans with lower sone ratings usually are more expensive than those with high ratings.

This project features a 6-inch diameter axial fan with a rating of 270 cfm and 2.5 sones. Six-inch diameter flexible ducts connect two air inlets—one over the tub and the other over the toilet—to the motor and the vent system. The system exits to an outside wall about 5 feet from the fan. The exit is capped with a metal hood. For most houses, cutting the existing siding is not a problem. For masonry or stucco, however, the estimate should include another 2 hours of labor at $60 per hour.

Electrical connections need to be made by a licensed electrician who is familiar with local codes. Some building codes specify that fans and overhead light fixtures be on the same switch. Other codes dictate that a fan with an infrared heater be connected to a separate 20-amp circuit.

Cost for materials = $377

Total contractor's fee including materials = $782

Understairs
Clothes Closet

The area under the stairs often is unused space. Turning this space into a closet yields a significant amount of storage area. For maximum doorway height, plan the closet door at the end of the stairway, parallel to the stairs. If there isn't enough height to allow a normal 6-foot, 8-inch door, you may have to install a modified door. A modified door may require framing a corner of the doorway at an angle, then cutting the door to match.

Use the lower portions of the space for storing bulky items. Because this space may be awkward to access, plan this area for long-term storage of items. Where the closet is more upright, install a clothes pole for hanging garments.

In this project, the triangular space under the edge of the stairs is enclosed with a stud wall. The interior and exterior of the wall are finished with drywall. For about the same price, you may prefer to finish the insides of the closet wall with cedar particle board. The undersides of the stairs can be coated with leftover paint or left unfinished.

Cost for materials = $302

Total contractor's fee including materials = $799

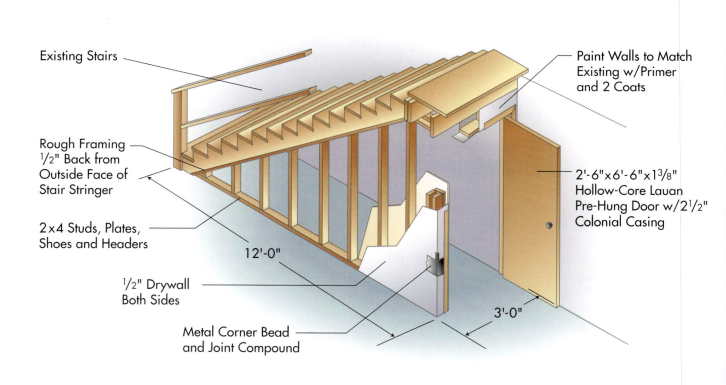

Existing Stairs

Rough Framing
1/2" Back from
Outside Face of
Stair Stringer

2x4 Studs, Plates,
Shoes and Headers

12'-0"

1/2" Drywall
Both Sides

Metal Corner Bead
and Joint Compound

Paint Walls to Match
Existing w/Primer
and 2 Coats

2'-6"x6'-6"x1³/₈"
Hollow-Core Lauan
Pre-Hung Door w/2¹/₂"
Colonial Casing

3'-0"

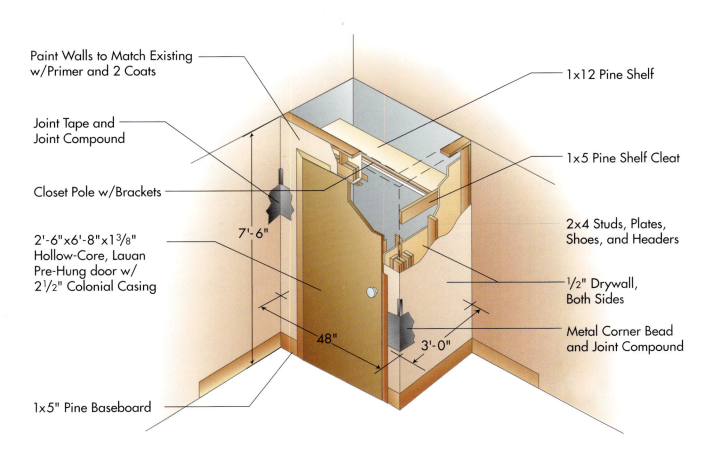

Paint Walls to Match Existing w/Primer and 2 Coats

Joint Tape and Joint Compound

Closet Pole w/Brackets

2'-6"x6'-8"x1 3/8" Hollow-Core, Lauan Pre-Hung door w/ 2 1/2" Colonial Casing

7'-6"

48"

1x5" Pine Baseboard

1x12 Pine Shelf

1x5 Pine Shelf Cleat

2x4 Studs, Plates, Shoes, and Headers

1/2" Drywall, Both Sides

3'-0"

Metal Corner Bead and Joint Compound

Standard
Clothes
Closet

Closets are high on the list of any home's most desirable features. A basement closet is useful for seasonal storage of clothing or as an addition to a lower-level bedroom. This 48x30-inch project fits into an existing corner and requires only the construction of two stud walls. Drywall is applied to both the interior and exterior of the stud walls for a completely finished appearance. The project includes a shelf for supplemental storage and a clothes pole with support brackets.

Many door styles are available for closets. This example uses a hollow core interior door. Louvered doors encourage air circulation within the closet and are preferred if your basement tends to be musty and have high humidity. To protect clothes from stale odors, place a desiccant within the closet to trap excess humidity.

The closet is installed in a finished room directly over existing flooring, so no new flooring is specified. Stud walls are attached to joists overhead and a drywall ceiling installed.

Cost for materials = $449
Total contractor's fee including materials = $1,172

Laundry Center

If your basement plans call for fully finished rooms, you may want to place the washer and dryer in their own hideaway location, complete with folding doors.

This 6x3-foot project places the major appliances side-by-side inside a closet-type enclosure. A 5-foot-wide, bifold door assures complete access to both machines, and a built-in shelf offers storage for detergent boxes, bleach bottles, and other laundry aids. A 4-foot-long fluorescent light fixture, hung on the ceiling, provides plenty of light. The stud walls have drywall on the inside and outside. With the door closed, the enclosure helps reduce noise generated by the machines.

The enclosure must have access to hot and cold water supply pipes, a drain system, and electrical outlets. It should be located on an exterior wall so that the dryer can be properly vented to the out-side. Although not required by code, it's a good idea to locate your laundry facilities near a floor drain to handle any overflows or leaks.

The distance a dryer can be located from an exterior wall is usually limited to about an 8-foot run of vent pipe. Bringing water and electrical hookups to the laundry should not be a problem, but accessing a drain system may be. The problem with drains is allowing the proper amount of "fall" for new drain pipe so that the drain system remains compliant with standard building codes. Consult a plumbing professional about locating a drain. Sometimes, washers and dryers can be installed on a platform that conceals part of the drain line and permits some flexibility with location of the laundry facilities.

Cost for materials = $609
Total contractor's fee including materials = $1,528

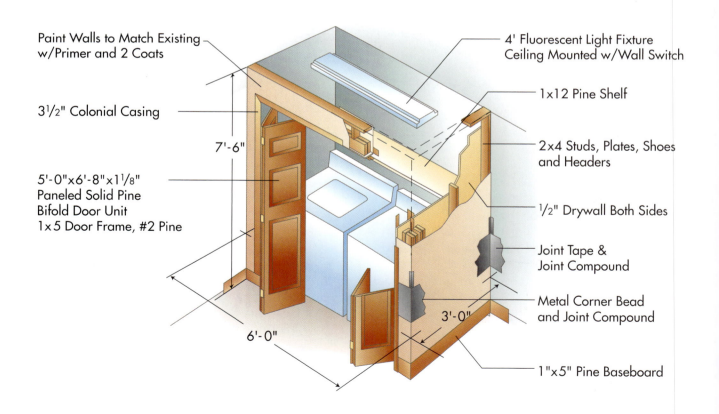

Paint Walls to Match Existing w/Primer and 2 Coats

3½" Colonial Casing

7'-6"

5'-0"x6'-8"x1⅛" Paneled Solid Pine Bifold Door Unit
1x5 Door Frame, #2 Pine

6'-0"

4' Fluorescent Light Fixture Ceiling Mounted w/Wall Switch

1x12 Pine Shelf

2x4 Studs, Plates, Shoes and Headers

½" Drywall Both Sides

Joint Tape & Joint Compound

Metal Corner Bead and Joint Compound

3'-0"

1"x5" Pine Baseboard

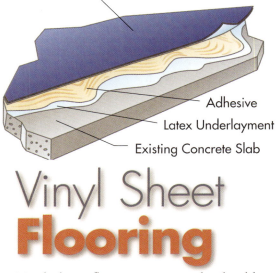

New Vinyl Sheetgoods

Adhesive

Latex Underlayment

Existing Concrete Slab

Vinyl Sheet Flooring

Vinyl sheet flooring is a tough, durable material well-suited to covering concrete slab floors. There are many styles, textures, and colors to choose from, and a variety of prices. The material you select should be the kind that is installed with adhesive or adhesive tape. Some varieties require the edges to be stapled to the subfloor. If your flooring is to be installed over concrete, staples won't work.

Most vinyl sheet flooring can be installed over old sheet goods, vinyl tiles, and wood flooring as long as the old flooring is clean and free of cracks, chips, or other imperfections. If old vinyl flooring has an embossed pattern, it may show through the new flooring. Ask your flooring dealer for advice about installing new vinyl over existing materials.

This 11x11.5-foot project uses a high-quality, .08-inch-thick vinyl sheet goods and includes the cost of removing old baseboard and painting and installing new pine baseboard.

Cost for materials = $502

Total contractor's fee including materials = $1,083

Frame and Finish Partition Wall

Partition walls are not load-bearing and can be constructed almost anywhere you want them. In basements, care must be taken to make sure the bottom plate is level. If the basement floor slopes toward a drain, the wall will have to be shimmed level, or the studs cut at different lengths to compensate for the slope. To protect against possible damage caused by dampness, the bottom plate should be pressure-treated wood to resist mold and rot.

The cost of this 10x7'8"-high wall includes a pre-hung, hollow-core door with casing and a doorknob. If you plan a partition wall without a door, subtract about 15 percent of the total contractor's fee.

Cost for materials = $411

Total contractor's fee including materials = $992

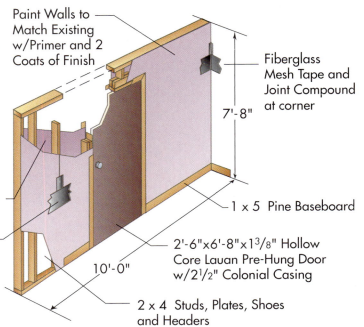

Paint Walls to Match Existing w/Primer and 2 Coats of Finish

Fiberglass Mesh Tape and Joint Compound at corner

7'-8"

1 x 5 Pine Baseboard

2'-6"x6'-8"x1³/₈" Hollow Core Lauan Pre-Hung Door w/2¹/₂" Colonial Casing

1/2" Drywall Both Sides

Fiberglass Mesh Tape and Joint Compound at all Seams

10'-0"

2 x 4 Studs, Plates, Shoes and Headers

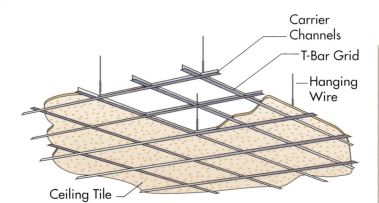

Carrier Channels

T-Bar Grid

Hanging Wire

Ceiling Tile

Suspended Ceiling

With its ability to hide exposed joists, plumbing pipes, ductwork, and electrical wires, a suspended ceiling is one of the most popular basement projects. The ceiling is economical, installs easily, and offers some sound insulation. The ceiling tiles are removable, allowing easy access for repairs or modifications to your home's systems. As an added benefit, the system hides overhead joists that are bowed or sagging.

A suspended ceiling consists of lightweight acoustical tiles shaped either as 2x2-foot squares or 2x4-foot rectangles. The tiles fit in a metal grid system that is hung by wires from the overhead joists. The grid system is installed first, and then the tiles. The grid must be hung at least 3 inches below the lowest point in the ceiling to allow for installation of the tiles. Calculate the distance from the finished ceiling to the floor to ensure you'll have adequate headroom once the work is complete.

Some systems include clear or translucent acrylic panels that can be fitted under light fixtures that are mounted to the joists. This 21x23-foot project includes four luminous panels, but not the light fixtures themselves. For lighting, consider fluorescent fixtures. They are relatively flat and easy to install against exposed joists.

Cost for materials = $659

Total contractor's fee including materials = $1,967

Adjusting Costs to Your Location

The costs described in this chapter are based on national averages for labor and materials. To adjust these figures for your location, multiply the cost shown in each project by the factor given in this table.

Alabama
Birmingham	.84
Mobile	.83
Montgomery	.82

Alaska
Anchorage	1.27
Fairbanks	1.27
Juneau	1.26

Arizona
Flagstaff	.95
Phoenix	.93
Tucson	.91

Arkansas
Little Rock	.81
Hot Springs	.71
Pine Bluff	.80

California
Bakersfield	1.11
Los Angeles	1.11
Oakland	1.16
Pasadena	1.08
Berkeley	1.29
Sacramento	1.12

Colorado
Boulder	.90
Denver	.98
Colorado Springs	.93
Durango	.89

Connecticut
Hartford	1.05
Bridgeport	1.02
New London	1.06

Delaware
Newark	.99
Wilmington	.98
Dover	.99

District of Columbia
Washington	.94

Florida
Miami	.86
Tampa Bay	.83
Tallahassee	.78

Georgia
Atlanta	.84
Columbus	.80
Dalton	.64

Hawaii
Honolulu	1.27
Hilo	1.27

Idaho
Boise	.95
Twin Falls	.82
Lewiston	1.11

Illinois
Chicago	1.12
Rockford	1.03
Peoria	1.07
Carbondale	.96

Indiana
Indianapolis	.97
South Bend	.92
Terra Haute	.95

Iowa
Des Moines	.96
Cedar Rapids	.99
Spencer	.83

Kansas
Kansas City	.95
Colby	.88
Wichita	.89

Kentucky
Lexington	.89
Bowling Green	.94
Somerset	.77

Louisiana
New Orleans	.87
Alexandria	.79
Shreveport	.81

Maine
Portland	.89
Bangor	.93
Waterville	.81

Maryland
Annapolis	.90
Salisbury	.79
Baltimore	.92

Massachusetts
Boston	1.16
Worcester	1.12
Pittsfield	1.01

Michigan
Detroit	1.06
Bay City	.95
Grand Rapids	.91

Minnesota
Minneapolis	1.14
Duluth	1.03
Bemidji	.91

Mississippi
Jackson	.83
Meridian	.78
Biloxi	.85

Missouri
St. Louis	.99
Columbia	.96
Springfield	.85

Montana
Billings	.98
Missoula	.95
Kalispell	.94

Nebraska
Omaha	.90
Grand Island	.88
Alliance	.77

Nevada
Las Vegas	1.04
Reno	.94
Elko	.93

New Hampshire
Manchester	.96
Claremont	.80
Portsmouth	.95

New Jersey
Vineland	1.11
Atlantic City	1.11
Newark	1.15

New Mexico
Albuquerque	.89
Santa Fe	.89
Roswell	.89

New York
Staten Island	1.29
Queens	1.28
Albany	.98
Syracuse	1.01
Buffalo	1.08

North Carolina
Wilmington	.75
Greensboro	.78
Raleigh	.79

North Dakota
Fargo	.79
Bismark	.81
Minot	.81

Ohio
Cleveland	1.08
Columbus	.96
Cincinnati	.98
Marion	.91

Oklahoma
Oklahoma City	.81
Tulsa	.86
Guymon	.70

Oregon
Portland	1.09
Eugene	1.06
Klamath Falls	1.06

Pennsylvania
Pittsburgh	1.05
Philadelphia	1.12
Scranton	.97
Oil City	.90

Rhode Island
| Newport | 1.04 |
| Providence | 1.04 |

South Carolina
Columbia	.74
Charleston	.76
Rock Hill	.66

South Dakota
Sioux Falls	.89
Pierre	.87
Rapid City	.86

Tennessee
Nashville	.85
Memphis	.86
Cookeville	.70

Texas
Dallas	.91
Lubbock	.80
Houston	.89
Austin	.80

Utah
Salt Lake City	.88
Provo	.89
Price	.83

Vermont
Montpelier	.84
Brattleboro	.76
Burlington	.85

Virginia
Norfolk	.85
Richmond	.85
Roanoke	.79

Washington
Seattle	1.00
Spokane	1.01
Wenatchee	.97

West Virginia
Charleston	.94
Clarksburg	.97
Martinsburg	.78

Wisconsin
Milwaukee	1.01
Madison	.97
Green Bay	.99

Wyoming
Cheyenne	.88
Casper	.88
Worland	.81

Working With A Contractor

Unless you are an accomplished do-it-yourselfer with plenty of time to devote to a project, you will probably need to hire a professional building contractor. Selecting a contractor is one of the most important aspects of getting your project done to your satisfaction. Take the time necessary to choose a contractor who has a good reputation and who is someone you feel comfortable with.

A licensed contractor is one who has completed state requirements to perform various types of work. General contractors have a broad knowledge of all aspects of construction and are hired to organize and complete a job according to an agreed-upon schedule. Other contractors, called subcontractors, have a more specific area of expertise. Electrical contractors, for example, have passed a state certification program that permits them to perform work relating to electrical hookups. It is your general contractor's responsibility to hire all subcontractors necessary to complete your project. A good general contractor has established relationships with many reliable subcontractors and can be counted on to furnish quality work that is completed in a timely fashion.

Hiring a Contractor

To find a qualified general contractor:

■ Ask friends, neighbors, colleagues, or professional acquaintances for names of reliable contractors. Make sure you have several recommendations to choose from.

■ Meet with prospective contractors to discuss your project. Ask about their experience remodeling basements and what problems they have encountered. Don't hesitate to ask for a "ballpark" figure for your particular project. A ballpark figure isn't a precise bid and you should not regard it as an agreement of any kind. Discussing money, however, will give you some idea of how knowledgeable contractors are and how comfortable they will be when it comes to talking about specific costs.

Also ask them how long they have been in business, and if they carry insurance. Without insurance, you are liable for any accidents that occur on your property. Most contractors have a certificate of insurance. It is an acceptable part of the process to request that you see the certificate before proceeding. A contractor should have insurance to cover damage, liability, and worker's compensation.

Gauge your interaction carefully. How you feel about a prospective contractor is an important factor in deciding who will get the job.

■ Obtain references from contractors and take the time to inspect their work. Reliable contractors should provide this information readily and will be proud to have their work on display. Check with your local Better Business Bureau to see if any complaints have been filed about your candidates.

■ Narrow your choices—select three to five contractors—and ask for final bids. Make sure all contractors have similar deadlines for submitting bids—about three weeks should be sufficient. Eliminate from contention any contractor who posts a late bid without a reasonable excuse; having too much work is not a valid excuse.

■ Review each bid carefully to see how thoroughly the bids have been researched. A bid should include itemized lists of materials, itemized figures for installation work, a timeline with stages of completion clearly defined, and an amount specified for the contractor's fee—usually 10 to 15 percent of the total costs. The best contractors will offer a penalty for work that is not completed in a reasonable amount of time. There also should be an agreed-upon rate for change orders. Change orders occur when you decide to make alterations to the plan or to the type of materials specified. Although most contractors will work hand-in-hand with clients to make minor changes, some alterations cause work delays that disrupt shipping arrangements or cause a contractor to alter schedules with other jobs. The best way to avoid changes is to plan thoroughly, well in advance.

■ When it comes to final selection, take all factors into account, including price. Be skeptical of any bid that seems quite a bit lower than others— the lowest bidder is not always the one who will give the most satisfying results.

■ Once you find your contractor, you should make an effort to keep lines of communication open. Schedule regular meetings to discuss progress and keep informed of interim deadlines. Tell your contractor that you don't expect to make your final payment until the job has passed all required building inspections, you have seen written proof that all subcontractors and suppliers have been paid, and you and your contractor have walked through the project and agreed that the job is complete.

Getting Bids

Creating bids for your project is not just the job of your prospective contractors—you have some responsibilities, too. Your primary responsibility will be to furnish detailed blueprint drawings and a complete materials list. Blueprints usually are produced by a registered architect, but a qualified designer or even the homeowner can create usable plans. Blueprints from a registered architect can be given directly to a contractor for bids, but plans produced by a designer or the homeowner must first be reviewed, approved, and stamped by a registered structural engineer.

The materials list should be as complete and comprehensive as possible. It should specify the quantity and brand names of materials needed, and the brand names and model numbers of fixtures and appliances that are to be installed. If specific companies are not identified, then the contractor will furnish brands he or she is familiar with.

Many homeowners enjoy being involved in the selection process and like to shop for specialty items themselves. Be sure your contractor understands your intentions and the materials list indicates any purchases you intend to make. Both you and your contractor must agree about any possible limitations due to size, weight, and other relevant factors.

When bids start to arrive, study them to see how each was prepared and the level of detail each contractor provides. A meticulously prepared bid usually indicates that the contractor has given careful consideration to your project and is prepared for potential problems. If all the bids vary widely, you should review each bid with the contractor who prepared it to discover reasons why. It may be that certain items or tasks have been omitted. Make sure all the prospective contractors are working with identical information about your plans. A contractor maybe willing to resubmit another bid based on new criteria or information.

Making a Contract

Once you have made your selection, you should sign a written contract with your contractor. Many contractors have prepared contract forms. If you are unsure about the specific points of a contract, you should consult with an attorney before proceeding to sign any document.

Contracts are not all alike, but a good contract should cover the following points:

■ A precise description of all work to be completed by the contractor and subcontractors, and a description all materials that are to be installed.

■ The total cost of the job, including all materials, labor, and fees.

■ A schedule of payments that you will make to the contractor. Be wary of contracts asking for large up-front payments—some states even limit the amount of up-front payments made to contractors before work begins.

■ A work schedule with calendar dates specified for the completion of each stage of the project. The schedule should include an allowance for delays due to delivery problems, weather-related interruptions, and back orders of scarce products.

■ A "right of recision" that allows the homeowner to back out of the contract within 72 hours of signing.

■ A certificate of insurance that guarantees the contractor has the appropriate insurance.

■ A warranty that guarantees that the labor and materials are free from defects for a certain period of time, usually one year.

■ An arbitration clause that specifies a method that you and your contractor will use to settle any disputes about materials, quality, or charges.

■ A description of change-order procedures stating what will happen if you decide to make alterations to the plans or specifications after the contract has been signed. The description should include a fee structure for change requests.

■ A release of liens that assures homeowners they won't incur liens or charges against their property as a result of legal actions filed against the contractor or any of the subcontractors.

Numbers in **bold** indicate pages with photographs.